THE
KINGDOM
FOCUSED
LEADER

THE
KINGDOM
FOCUSED
LEADER

SEEING GOD AT WORK
IN *you*,
THROUGH *you*,
& AROUND *you*

MICHAEL D. MILLER

BROADMAN
&HOLMAN
PUBLISHERS

NASHVILLE, TENNESSEE

0–8054–3151–9

Published by Broadman & Holman Publishers
Nashville, Tennessee

Dewey Decimal Classification: 231.72
Subject Heading: KINGDOM OF GOD—GROWTH

1 2 3 4 5 6 7 8 9 10 08 07 06 05 04

To Ed Green

Contents

Preface

You are reading these words because you are a leader or have some interest in leadership. I wrote this book with you in mind. My calling, my passion is to help other natural-born leaders to lead at full capacity and to focus this work on kingdom priorities.

There is a leadership concept that I have discovered on the journey that I believe will benefit you if you can grasp it. If you can get this one thing it will change your life. It's not new. In fact it's been around for centuries. It is tried and true, yet largely unknown to leaders and rarely tested. The truth that can change your life is the reality of the kingdom of God. Yes, that's right, the kingdom of God.

All leaders share the ability to see the big picture. Not all leaders are visionaries, but all true leaders see the big picture. The kingdom of God is the ultimate, IMAX, three-dimensional perspective of life from God's perspective. It is a present reality in which we live our lives and conduct our business.

As you read the pages of this book, I pray that you will discover the power of kingdom focus in your leadership role. Let God work in you, through you, and around you to do great things for His glory.

Many people have helped me along my own journey toward becoming a kingdom-focused leader. First, I must thank my wife Pat. She is my best friend and constant supporter. I would also like to thank my good friend and partner in kingdom work, Gene Mims.

This book was possible because of the help of several people. I would like to thank Chris Johnson and Bill Seaver for their long hours of work on this project. Thanks also to John Kramp, who challenged me to write this book. I am better for the work! Finally, I must thank my assistant, Christy Burch, whose help made this book a reality.

1

What's a Leader to Do?

I'm a leader and I'm a Christian, but there's got to be something more!" That's how my conversation with Bob began. He explained, "Mike, I am a little frustrated. I love working at the church, serving on committees, and teaching Sunday school. I serve as a trustee for our Christian college, but I feel like I am not using all my leadership gifts and business skills for God!"

Bob is a successful businessman. He came to know Christ during college. He thought he was called to be a minister, but after a brief time working on a church staff, he realized that kind of work was not for him. He became a successful businessman and was vice president of an oil company for a number of years. Since then he has started a number of businesses.

As a Christian entrepreneur, Bob has been blessed by God with great business sense. He is also a strong community leader, with many in his city calling on him for business advice. His leadership gifts are evident to everyone. But as we spoke, he seemed frustrated and confused. Have you ever felt like this?

You've picked up this book because you are a leader. If you are like me, you have read many different leadership books. Bob's words at the beginning of this chapter expressed the frustration of a friend who was trying to determine how his work as a successful business leader connected with his faith in Christ.

Now back to Bob's story.

I leaned forward in my chair and said, "Bob, I want you to think about something that you may never have considered. It is a big picture perspective, bigger than you or me. You're not just a church leader or a successful Christian business-man. You are a kingdom leader! God has created and gifted you to help extend His kingdom through your business life! The most awesome reality in the universe is the kingdom of God. And God has determined to build His kingdom through people like you!" Bob thought for a moment and then asked, "What is a kingdom leader?"

Bob had never really thought much about the kingdom of God. He said, "I've heard you mention the kingdom of God, but I really never thought that it had anything to do with me. I've always considered the kingdom of God as something that is coming in the future. Right now we are down here just struggling along, waiting and looking for our chance to go to heaven. In fact, I have always thought that the kingdom of God was all about heaven. So what does the kingdom of God have to do with me as a business leader?"

➤ ➤ ➤

There is an amazing similarity between Bob and many other leaders in business, athletics, government, and church life. Many Christian leaders do not understand the present reality of the kingdom of God. Gene Mims, in *The Kingdom-Focused Church*, describes the kingdom of God in this way:

> The kingdom of God is the reign of God in today's world. The kingdom is the ultimate reality and sovereign movement of God in the universe. This is expressed in the transforming truth that Jesus Christ rules over all things and is evidenced by God's supernatural work in and through believers in local churches. The kingdom of God must be the central life focus that every person should seek and align with in order to know the full and abundant life God created people to experience in Christ.[1]

Charles Swindoll gives this explanation of the kingdom of God. "God's kingdom is a synonym for God's rule. Those who choose to live in His kingdom (those still very much alive on Planet Earth) choose to live under His authority. . . . [This is] His rightful authority over our lives."[2]

Many Christian leaders do not understand the concept of the kingdom of God and their role in extending God's kingdom throughout the world. They struggle with real meaning related to their jobs. They wonder if what they do on a daily basis really contributes to God's purposes in our world. Often they feel like second-class Christians because they are not serving on a church staff.

Bob Buford, a successful businessman and author of *Halftime: Changing Your Game Plan from Success to Significance and Game Plan: Winning Strategies for the Second Half of Your Life,* understands the significant role of believers in the workplace. He is the founder of Leadership Network, a nonprofit organization created to encourage innovation and entrepreneurship among leaders of large churches and parachurch organizations, and Faith Works, an organization promoting partnerships between marketplace leaders and faith-based organizations.

"One of the most common characteristics of a person nearing the end of the first half of life," says [Buford] with conviction, "is that unquenchable desire to move from success to significance. After a first half of doing what we're supposed to do, we would like to do something in the second half that's more meaningful—something rising above the perks and paychecks into the stratosphere of significance. And significance comes when you find a way to give yourself to God."

This growing desire led Buford to make some major changes in [his life}. He didn't sell his business or give away his money and become a minister, but he did redirect his abilities and energies toward different goals.

"For me, the logic of this allegiance led me to stay involved with my business, functioning as a rear-echelon chairman of the board and devoting about 20 percent of my time to setting the vision and values of the company, picking key executives, setting standards, and monitoring performance. The remaining 80 percent of my time was given over to an array of other things, most of which centered on leadership development for churches and nonprofit organizations—serving those who serve others, helping them be more effective in their work."

This orientation grows out of Buford's mission for his second half: "To transform the latent energy in American Christianity into active energy."[3]

I want to share with you a wonderful challenge. As a Christian leader, you must first understand the reality of the kingdom of God and then begin to live as a kingdom-focused leader! Learning and practicing these two things can radically alter your life as a leader. It can bring great fulfillment and meaning to your life. Understanding and focusing your life on the kingdom of God can dramatically change your self-confidence and satisfaction in your current leadership role.

Over the past few years I have observed how God has placed a group of specially called and assigned born-again leaders throughout the world to participate in extending His kingdom work! They serve in all kinds of industries. These gifted leaders have the potential to make an incredible impact on their world for Christ. Not only are they successful leaders, but they also seek to live out their faith in their positions of leadership.

Truett Cathy, founder of Chick-fil-A, is an example of a successful businessman who lives out his faith in the marketplace.

"[Truett] looks not to himself as the main benefactor in his life but to a much higher influence that still shapes his world and the business of Chick-fil-A. Cathy's policy of operating six days a week and leaving the Lord's Day to be observed in worship, or whatever forms of leisure his employees choose, has been questioned. His firm stance has not wavered. We don't expect all our operators to be Christian,' he said, 'but we do expect them to operate on biblical principles. We have a diverse mixture in our crew, but we haven't had any conflict as far as religious practices go."

At headquarters we have a devotional time once a week with about one hundred folks attending," says Bubba. "We have a music team and we sing and pray together. It's optional but Dad, Dan, Jimmy, and I make it a priority. At our corporate meeting in San Diego a few years ago, Dad gave each of our 700 operators a framed copy of Jeremiah 29:11: "For I know the plans I have for you," declares the LORD, 'plans to prosper you and not to harm you, plans to give you hope and a future.'" We believe this about Chick-fil-A."[4]

Sadly, however, many of these Christian leaders don't appreciate the value of their influence as leaders in their places of work. I am amazed when I talk with Christian leaders about their leadership influence for the kingdom. They often say they feel the need to quit their jobs and join a church staff or do more with their church rather than serve as leaders where they currently work. Don't get me wrong. It is vital that every believer have a ministry in the local church. But God does not want these leaders to miss the opportunity to be good stewards of their God-given leadership gifts right where they work.

Dallas Willard notes that "it is as great and as difficult a spiritual calling to run the factories and the mines, the banks and the department stores, the schools and the government agencies for the kingdom of God as it is to pastor a church or serve as an evangelist. There truly is no division between sacred and secular except what we have created."[5]

Many of these leaders act as if they have an inferiority complex. They don't recognize the awesome opportunities they have to contribute to kingdom work while serving in their current positions. These leaders are under the mistaken impression that the kingdom of God is only about the church. But the kingdom is also about God being at work in the real world where they work and live.

As Bob and I continued to talk, I said, "Bob, don't you see the position God has put you in? He has placed you among people and organizations that your pastor would never have the opportunity to reach. You have built a worldwide network of people whom you can call upon for help on any number of issues and who look to you as a spiritual person. You underestimate your importance to God as a kingdom leader!

"You see, Bob, God does His kingdom work *in* you, *through* you, and *around* you! The kingdom of God is not just a future hope. It is a present reality that changes us on the inside and works its way out through our lives. Our job is to focus on God's kingdom work in these three dimensions, as He works *in* us, *through* us, and *around* us.

"God is at work *in* you, and His kingdom is a present reality when Jesus is Lord of your life. His mission is to transform you to become just like Him and to produce the fruit of the Spirit in you. At the same time, God is working *through* you. You are His instrument to do His work in the world. God works through you to make a difference in the world by being salt and light and to point people to Jesus. He wants to work through you to impact the people in your sphere of influence for the kingdom of God. God is working in you and through you, but at the same time He is always at work *around* you. Kingdom-focused leaders are always alert to what God is doing around them so that they can join Him in His kingdom work."

Bob sat back and shook his head. He finally said, "Wow! Mike, you have really challenged me to think in a new way. Tell me some more about this kingdom stuff. You are starting to give me hope that God might really want to use me for His purposes through what I do all week long."

If you are a Christian and a leader, regardless of your current place of service, I want to encourage you to develop a kingdom focus. It is important that you come to see the three dimensions of a kingdom reality. When you, a Christian leader, have that kind of focus, it radically changes how you view yourself, your work, and your world.

So what qualifies me to write to you about this kind of truth? Well, I, too, am a Christian leader. I have served as a church leader; I have been a pastor and church staff member. Now I serve as a leader in a Christian not-for-profit publishing company. I, too, have had to struggle with the value of my current work.

I have often wondered, since I no longer serve on a church staff, if my work is as important as what I used to do as a pastor. When I start thinking like that, I lose my focus on the work that God has called me to do now. I forget that God has sent me to do my work as a kingdom leader in this job just as He assigned me to be a pastor in the past. Bottom line: my current work is just as significant as my work as a pastor. It is all a matter of my focus on the kingdom of God revealed *in* me, *through* me, and *around* me.

In the past few years I have learned some wonderful truths from God's Word about the kingdom of God. Before this time I never fully grasped the kingdom as a reality that affected all of my life. God has been teaching me about this larger kingdom reality and my place in it. I have many great friends like Bob who are searching for the key to making sense out of what they are doing as leaders. I felt motivated to write this book to offer encouragement to Christian leaders in the marketplace.

If you are like me, searching for meaning and purpose in what you are now doing for God, I hope you will find this book helpful. It is written to provide you, as a leader, with encouragement in your current calling from God. I challenge you to think in a new way about your leadership. What I said to my friend Bob is true for you: You are a kingdom leader! Your great challenge as a Christian is to be a leader who is focused on what God is doing in you, through you, and around you.

The first and most important thing for a kingdom-focused leader is a clear understanding of the reality of the kingdom of God. Let's think about the awesome reality of the kingdom of God for a few minutes.

2

The Big Picture— the Kingdom of God

When I think of my conversation with Bob, I recall how he challenged me to explain the kingdom in terms he could understand. As we continued our conversation in Bob's office, we began to talk about the fact that leaders understand the "big picture." Whatever it may be called in the leadership books, leaders see the big picture. They carry a vision of the future that others cannot see. Leaders guide their organizations to attempt great things because they have been captivated by a big idea or big dream!

I have been interested in astronomy for many years. When I was a boy, my mother took me to the library where I was drawn to books that captured those mysterious, beautiful pictures and stories about the stars. Astronomy gives us a perspective and understanding about our universe. It reveals the awesome vastness and expansiveness of the universe, while establishing our place in the cosmos.

One writer describes the cosmos, or universe, as "the whole of material reality, all the way from the macro, or very large, to and through the middle range, to the micro, or very small."[1] The sheer size of the universe is staggering to comprehend: "Astronomers have determined that the total universe contains no less than 100 billion trillion stars, adhered by gravity into various-shaped galaxies and clusters."[2]

So why this astronomy lesson, and what does it have to do with leadership? There are strong parallels between the universe and the kingdom of God. The universe is the present reality in which we live and move and breathe, but the kingdom of God is just as real! As leaders we must learn to understand and appreciate the truth that we live within the powerful reality of the kingdom!

Like the universe, the kingdom of God, to use the astronomer's language, is from macro to micro in size! Kingdom reality starts at the micro level within the heart of a believer as Jesus Christ rules as Lord of his or her life. But the kingdom is also as vast as the entire created order. It is vast and all-encompassing, massive and growing! A kingdom leader understands this reality!

How does the cosmos relate to thinking about vision? There is an invisible dynamic in much of the cosmos. From the micro perspective, we do not see atoms and molecules, but we know they exist. From a macro perspective we don't see the wind, but we see the results of the wind. We don't see all of the planets of the Milky Way, yet we know they exist. We don't see the kingdom of God, for it is an invisible kingdom, but we know it exists. Having vision is the ability to see or visualize the unseen. Being a kingdom-focused leader means you have a vision of the unseen reality of God at work in you, through you, and around you, and you help others to visualize or accept by faith what they cannot see.

A copy of an ancient letter tells the following story: The coliseum was packed, the crowd thirsty for blood. Several men and women were roughly herded into the center of the arena. One sympathetic guard whispered to the trembling group: "Lions seldom attack people who remain tightly grouped together."

Suddenly, four intentionally starved lions sprang from their opened cages and began circling their prey. The group of Christians huddled more tightly together. But as a huge lion approached one side, a young pregnant woman stumbled and fell forward. The lion immediately pounced, dragging the young woman and her unborn child to a gruesome death.

Even in the face of this unspeakable horror, those Christians who remained carefully sank to their knees, lifted their faces to heaven, and began to sing a song of faith and hope. As their voices rose to the ears of the Roman general in charge of the event, he solemnly asked a question of no one in particular: "How is it that these Christians can look into the very abyss of death and yet sing songs of faith and hope?"

A young soldier named Adrianis who had, unknown to the general and others in the coliseum, become a Christian himself while working in the Christian-filled dungeons, answered quietly, "They say, sir, that it is because of unseen things that they see."

Think with me for a moment about what a kingdom-focused leader sees. It is not a fantasy or a hope but a reality. Kingdom-focused leaders live within the reality of God's kingdom. They are driven, compelled, and captivated by the reality of the kingdom of God! It is different from earthly kingdoms; though it is not often visible to the untrained eye, it exists, and it is growing.

If I had a dollar for every time that I have heard leadership gurus talk about the importance of vision, I would be a rich man! Leadership books teach that the leader is the giver of the vision that guides and empowers the organization. Experts on leadership often teach that an organization is only as good as the vision that guides it. They say if the leader lacks vision, the organization suffers. Leaders must see what others do not see. They must live in the world of vision and big ideas!

I don't know about you, but that puts great pressure on me as leader. I must somehow always be in touch with "the vision thing," or the organization I lead will be in trouble!

Vision is the big idea, the picture that every committed Christian leader must keep at the forefront of his mind. I am not talking about a vision that relates to how large your company, school, or church might be or how you can grow your business and increase revenues. But I want you to consider a vision of the present reality of the kingdom of God.

Kingdom-focused leaders have a vision God has given them for their work. For them the kingdom of God is the *present reality* in which they carry out their work. Remember, the kingdom of God is the rule of Jesus Christ expressed *in, through,* and *around* you.

A friend of mine often says that vision is imagining a future state. A kingdom-focused leader doesn't need to imagine a future state. Rather, he must keep his eyes open to the present reality of the kingdom of God. Paul said, "I pray that the eyes of your heart may be enlightened" (Eph. 1:18). The kingdom already exists. The better our understanding of the kingdom of God, the clearer our vision will be.

I remember sitting in a conference room listening to a group of speakers talk about the importance of understanding various worldviews. Speaker after speaker stressed the fact that the world is changing, the values and morals of society are in transition. I don't deny that it is vital for a leader to understand the various views that exist in the world in which we live and do our work. However, the kingdom of God shapes the worldview of the kingdom-focused leader.

Kingdom Facts

I want to challenge you to think about the kingdom of God. For some of you perhaps this is the first time that you have ever thought about the kingdom and its relationship to you as a leader. Others of you may have a keen understanding of the biblical facts about the lordship of Christ but have not stopped to apply that reality to your life and work.

As Christian leaders we must make the kingdom of God our *primary life focus.* Jesus said, "But seek first the kingdom of God and His righteousness, and all these things will be provided for you" (Matt. 6:33). Many times we get so caught up in worrying about our possessions, business, family, or personal pleasures that we forget that we have been called as believers to focus first on the kingdom of God.

There is no greater challenge for us as busy leaders than determining to make our first priority the pursuit of the kingdom of God. Jesus' promise to those who live with this focus is clear: "All these things will be provided for you." We can count on the Lord to take care of us when we seek first His kingdom and righteousness in our lives.

Fact 1: The Kingdom of God Is Growing and Cannot Be Stopped

The kingdom of God is *growing* and cannot be stopped. In Daniel 2:44, the prophet declared, "In the time of those kings, the God of heaven will set up a kingdom that will never be destroyed, nor will it be left to another people. It will crush all those kingdoms and bring them to an end, but it will itself endure forever" (NIV). When Jesus came preaching, He declared that this kingdom Daniel had spoken of had now come. He said, "Repent, because the kingdom of heaven has come near!" (Matt. 4:17). Jesus inaugurated the kingdom through His work on earth. He established the kingdom through His death on the cross. He now reigns as king of the kingdom of God. This eternal kingdom that Daniel predicted would come as a present reality.

A series of parables in Matthew 13 teach great truths about the kingdom of God. Jesus used parables about seed sprouting, growing, and producing a harvest to illustrate the kingdom's growth. In Matthew 13:24–30, the good seeds of the kingdom grew and produced a harvest in spite of the weeds among them. Jesus compared the kingdom to a mustard seed: "It's the smallest of all the seeds, but when grown, it's taller than the vegetables and becomes a tree, so that the birds of the sky come and nest in its branches" (Matt. 13:32).

When you consider that the kingdom of God is growing and cannot be stopped, your confidence grows. What is your leadership assignment today? As a Christian you are living in the reality of the ever-expanding and growing kingdom of God. Just take a look at any missionary magazine. You will see the advance of God's kingdom through people coming to know Christ as Lord and Savior. Truly we are living in a time of worldwide advancement of the kingdom of God. We are able to see this like no other generation before us.

Sadly, some leaders don't see the growth of the kingdom around them. Henry Blackaby, in his book *Experiencing God,* challenges us to "watch to see where God is working and join Him."[3] The kingdom-focused leader learns to see the world with spiritual eyes. To watch God's work in the world gives us confidence that no matter how terrible things may be, God is still at work growing His kingdom for His glory!

I have a friend who has worked for years in the oil industry. God has blessed him with great wealth. He faithfully supports mission causes. I asked him once why he was so willing to sacrifice and give his money for mission causes. He said, "Because I know that God is growing His kingdom as the gospel is preached and people come to know Christ around the world." He has always been an example to me of how a leader must maintain his focus on the growth of the kingdom of God.

Fact 2: The Kingdom of God Is a Present Reality

The kingdom of God is a *present reality,* not simply a spiritual ideal. The kingdom of God is real! You can see the movement and growth everywhere. Of course, the truths about the reality of the kingdom are mysterious to non-believers, but that does not make the kingdom any less real. Jesus has given believers the privilege of knowing the revealed truths of God's kingdom (Matt. 13:11). This kingdom can be *seen* (Mark 9:1; Luke 9:27; 19:11), *entered into* (Matt. 5:20; John 3:5), and *inherited* (Matt. 25:34).

Jesus said that the kingdom of God starts on the inside. He said, "The kingdom of God is within you" (Luke 17:21 NIV). So, as a Christian leader today, the reality of the kingdom begins by what God is doing inside your life.

When Jesus Christ is the boss of my life, several things will take place. I will determine to live my life under the lordship of Jesus Christ. I will continually seek the kingdom of God as a first priority in my life. Before I make decisions, I will seek to know and understand God's will and purpose for my life. I will live in the freedom Jesus Christ provides, not in bondage to my past sin and habits of life.

Because you are a leader, everyone is watching how you live. What you say, what you do, where you go—these things are being evaluated by others. When Christ reigns in our lives, we put away the old habits of life and follow Christ as committed disciples.

Jesus reminds us that only those who have *spiritual perception* can see and understand the reality of the kingdom of God (Matt. 13:9–17). As believers we have the wonderful privilege of seeing and understanding the great reality of the kingdom of God.

Fact 3: The Kingdom of God Is Infiltrating the World

We also should remember that the kingdom of God is *infiltrating* the world culture in which we live. Jesus said that the kingdom of God is like yeast in a loaf of bread (Matt. 13:33). When a baker is preparing to bake bread, he adds yeast to the mix. Though you cannot see the yeast at work, it mixes with the flour and infiltrates the entire composition of the bread that will be baked.

I have a friend who served as a lieutenant commander in the Navy for many years until recently retiring. He was assigned at one time in his career to work at the Naval Academy on the development of the leadership process used in their leadership training courses. We have talked about how exciting it is to see committed believers serve in the military at many different levels. These committed military leaders serve as kingdom-focused leaders throughout the world. They are like yeast mixed in with the flour in a loaf of bread. They have the opportunity to advance the kingdom of God from their assigned duties around the world.

Fact 4: The Kingdom of God Faces Hostile Spiritual Opposition

Jesus tells us that the kingdom of God is like a farmer who had a field of wheat that was sabotaged by an enemy who sowed weeds in with the wheat (Matt. 13:25).

Kingdom-focused leaders face a real enemy—Satan. The devil opposes the spread of the kingdom of God. He does everything within his limited power to sabotage the advancement of the kingdom.

Paul reminds us that "our battle is not against flesh and blood, but against the rulers, against the authorities, against the world powers of this darkness, against the spiritual forces of evil in the heavens" (Eph. 6:12). The kingdom of God advances against the kingdom of evil and darkness. The leader must recognize that the world, flesh, and the devil are all opposed to the advancement of the kingdom of God. We see signs of this reality throughout the world, even though we don't read or hear much about it on the news. There is greater persecution of Christians today than at any other time in history. That may surprise some, but it's true. It is strange that the enemies of God, those who fight to stop the advancement of the kingdom, have never learned that the persecution of believers does not stop the kingdom of God from growing. The words of Tertullian, a Christian leader, are still true today: "The blood of the martyrs is the seed of the Church."[4]

Satanic opposition to the growth of the kingdom is real and should not be overlooked. We protect ourselves from satanic attack when we put on the whole armor of God (Eph. 6:10–18).

> Finally, be strengthened by the Lord and by His vast strength. Put on the full armor of God so that you can stand against the tactics of the Devil. For our battle is not against flesh and blood, but against the rulers, against the authorities, against the world powers of this darkness, against the spiritual forces of evil in the heavens. This is why you must take up the full armor of God, so that you may be able to resist in the evil day, and having prepared everything, to take your stand. Stand, therefore,
>
> > with truth like a belt around your waist,
> > righteousness like armor on your chest,
> > and your feet sandaled with readiness for
> > > the gospel of peace.
> >
> > In every situation take the shield of faith,
> > and with it you will be able to extinguish
> > the flaming arrows of the evil one.
> > Take the helmet of salvation,
> > and the sword of the Spirit, which is God's
> > > word.
>
> With every prayer and request, pray at all times in the Spirit, and stay alert in this, with all perseverance and intercession for all the saints.

The best news about this opposition, however, is that no matter how hard the enemy tries to stop the advancement of the kingdom, he cannot do it. We are promised victory over the devil. Though sometimes he seems to be winning battles, the victory is already ours. Jesus guaranteed the victory when He died on the cross and inaugurated the kingdom with His blood. He said, "It is finished!" (John 19:30). The debt has been paid. Satan can never stop the growth of the kingdom.

Fact 5: The Kingdom of God Is of Great Value

We cannot miss one final fact about the kingdom. The kingdom of God is of greater *value* than anything else in the created world. As leaders we measure the effectiveness of people and processes by their ability to add value to our objectives.

Business leaders are interested in the bottom line. Sports leaders are searching for the most valuable players to take them to the championship. Pastors are seeking the most valuable methods of teaching the truth of God's Word to the church. No matter what your leadership assignment, every leader understands that *value* is of the utmost importance.

Jesus said that the kingdom is like a treasure hidden in a field (Matt. 13:44) or a pearl of great price (Matt. 13:45–46). When you discover that the kingdom of God is a reality, then, like the one who discovered the treasure or the pearl, you sell everything you have and hold on to the new treasure that you have discovered! Listen my fellow leader: nothing you possess can ever match the value of entering the kingdom of God and experiencing the kingdom's rule and reign in your personal life, which includes your role as a leader.

These are the facts. Nothing compares to the fact that the kingdom of God is real. It is the ultimate big picture. It frames all of our present existence. As kingdom-focused leaders we must seek the kingdom as the priority of our lives. We must understand that the kingdom is growing all around us. The kingdom is a present reality, not just a fantasy. This kingdom is infiltrating the world as we read these words. There is real spiritual opposition to the kingdom, but no created force that can stop the advance of the kingdom! And above all else, nothing compares to the value of the kingdom of God.

The kingdom begins in the hearts and lives of believers, working through them and affecting the world for God. As Christian leaders we have the obligation to live with a *kingdom focus.* Everything we do, every decision we make, every place we go should be determined with the advancement of the kingdom in mind. The kingdom of God *is* the big picture for the kingdom-focused leader.

3

Who's in Charge?

My friend Bob sat back in his office chair to think about the kingdom facts we had been discussing. I could tell something was on his mind. "So Bob, what do you think about all this kingdom stuff?" He looked at me and said, "As a Christian leader, I never considered that the kingdom of God was so important to me and my life.

"But in my business there is never a doubt about who is in charge of this company. My employees know that I make the decisions about our future. They understand that I have the clearest picture of our company's future. They know that I sign their paychecks. I assign them to their jobs, and they are accountable to me for the results. So who is in charge of the kingdom of God?" he asked with a smile.

I responded, "That is a great question. I am not surprised that you would ask such a question. I can answer it: Jesus Christ is in charge of the kingdom of God!"

Bob's question was about authority. Leadership is about authority. In any organization there is always a need to identify clearly who is the boss! Who sets the rules, and who determines the pace for the organization?

In this chapter I want you to consider Jesus Christ as the eternal leader of the kingdom of God, with the ultimate authority over it. Jesus is the Lord of all creation

because by Him everything was created,
in heaven and on earth, the visible and the
　invisible,
whether thrones or dominions or rulers or
　authorities—
all things have been created through Him and
　for Him.
He is before all things, and by Him all things
　hold together.
He is also the head of the body, the church;
He is the beginning, the firstborn from the
　dead,
so that He might come to have first place in
　everything (Col. 1:16–18).

The key phrases in this passage remind us that Jesus was involved in creation; all things were created by Him and for Him. He is the one who holds all things together, and all of this is revealed to us so that He will come to have His rightful place—first place in everything.

After the resurrection Jesus stood with His disciples and made this bold assertion: "All authority has been given to Me in heaven and on earth" (Matt. 28:18). The Father had given Him all authority. As the ruler of the kingdom of God, Jesus commissioned His followers to go to all the nations and make disciples. "Go, therefore, and make disciples of all nations, baptizing them in the name of the Father and of the Son and of the Holy Spirit, teaching them to observe everything I have commanded you. And remember, I am with you always, to the end of the age" (Matt. 28:19–20).

It is important to remember that Jesus commissioned His disciples. Perhaps you have served in the military. I have a friend who serves as a commissioned officer in the army. He works under the commander in chief. He is authorized to protect the Constitution of the United States. The president of the United States of America has the authority to commission him into active service for his country.

In the same way Jesus commissioned His disciples to advance the kingdom of God through worldwide evangelism. All believers have that same commission from the Lord. We must go and make disciples of all nations. As kingdom-focused leaders, we must never lose sight of our commission to go to the world and make disciples while we are engaged in our day-to-day work.

Jesus: Our Kingdom Leader

As you read these words, pause for a moment and realize that Jesus Christ is our kingdom leader. He is alive and guiding the work of advancing the kingdom of God. He is calling out leaders. He is freeing men and women from their sins. He is transforming our lives from day to day. He has given us the Holy Spirit to guide us and produce in us the fruit of the Spirit.

Some people talk about Jesus as if He were a distant historical figure. I laugh when I hear scholars talk about the "historic Jesus." He is alive today! The Bible tells us that He has ascended to heaven and now sits in the seat of highest honor! The Bible says of Jesus Christ, our kingdom leader:

> In these last days, He has spoken to us by His Son, whom He has appointed heir of all things and through whom He made the universe. He is the radiance of His glory, the exact expression of His nature, and He sustains all things by His powerful word. After making purification for sins, He sat down at the right hand of the Majesty on high. So He became higher in rank than the angels, just as the name He inherited is superior to theirs (Heb. 1:2–4).

Jesus Christ now is seated in the seat of highest honor in heaven. From that position of authority, He directs the affairs of His eternal kingdom. History is filled with kingdoms that have dominated the world. The Egyptian, Chinese, Greek, and Roman dynasties were great influences on the world at given times in history. But Jesus is king of a kingdom that is eternal, transcultural, and will never end!

The kingdom-focused leader understands that Jesus Christ is the king of the kingdom of God. He has all authority in heaven and earth. Everything that takes place in this world is working together to accomplish His purposes. There are no accidents or events that are not permitted by the Lord of the kingdom. He uses them to accomplish God's eternal purposes and to advance His kingdom (Rom. 8:28).

Keep in mind that Jesus Christ is our kingdom leader. You have the opportunity to lead your organization with the assurance that you are serving the Lord of the kingdom, who is in control of everything that is taking place in this world. He is not surprised by any event that takes place in this world. No government or event can stop the advancement of the kingdom of God!

Jesus: The Kingdom-Focused Leader

When I started working on a church staff many years ago, I worked with an older pastor who showed me the ropes. He modeled for me how a pastor is to do his work. His example helped me through the years to keep in perspective what is expected of a pastor of a church.

In the same way, Jesus is a model for all kingdom leaders of how we are to live and do our work. Every aspect of Jesus' life gives us an example that we can emulate. As kingdom-focused leaders, we are to be like Jesus. Philippians 2:5–11 tells us to have the same attitude that Jesus had by being more concerned for others than for our own selves. In coming to dwell among men, Jesus humbled Himself and took on humanity. He submitted Himself to the authority of God the Father. As Paul teaches us, though Jesus was God, He humbled Himself and came into this world under the authority of God the Father.

Make your own attitude that of Christ Jesus, who, existing in the form of God, did not consider equality with God as something to be used for His own advantage. Instead He emptied Himself by assuming the form of a slave, taking on the likeness of men. And when He had come as a man in His external form, He humbled Himself by becoming obedient to the point of death—even to death on a cross. For this reason God also highly exalted Him and gave Him the name that is above every name, so that at the name of Jesus every knee should bow—of those who are in heaven and on earth and under the earth—and every tongue should confess that Jesus Christ is Lord, to the glory of God the Father (Phil. 2:5–11).

Jesus' earthly ministry is an example of how we are to live as kingdom-focused leaders. His mission was clear. He was highly aware that God the Father had sent Him on a mission of salvation for the world. Jesus said: "The Son of Man has come to seek and to save the lost" (Luke 19:10). "For even the Son of Man did not come to be served, but to serve, and to give His life—a ransom for many" (Mark 10:45). Jesus came to this world under the authority of God the Father in order to accomplish this mission.

Jesus' perfect life models His unconditional response to God's call on His life. Hebrews 3:1 calls Jesus the apostle, one sent on a mission with the authority of the one who commissioned Him. The next verse declares that Jesus "was faithful to the One who appointed Him." God's call authorized and empowered Christ to accomplish the Father's purposes in the world.

Jesus responded to the authority of God the Father with single-mindedness, focus, and resolve that any kingdom-focused leader would do well to follow. He said only what God wanted Him to say, He did only the work that God wanted Him to do, and He went only where God wanted Him to go.

Jesus Said Only What God Wanted Him to Say

Jesus was conscious of His responsibility to speak only under the authority of God the Father. He said, "For I have not spoken on My own, but the Father Himself who sent Me has given Me a command as to what I should say and what I should speak" (John 12:49).

During His earthly ministry, Jesus focused on declaring the kingdom of God. The Bible tells us: "Jesus went to Galilee, preaching the good news of God: 'The time is fulfilled, and the kingdom of God has come near. Repent and believe in the good news!'" (Mark 1:14–15). He spoke over one hundred times about the kingdom of God and about the coming of the eternal kingdom of God through His mission on earth.

One of the most impressive things about Jesus during His earthly ministry was His ability to control His words. He had complete mastery of His tongue. Jesus always said just the right words for the right situation. At times He would not speak. At other times He would stand among the crowds and speak in a powerful way.

The words of a leader are very powerful. I have found in my current job, that my words can be used for good or bad. I recently met with one of my employees. I thought he was asking for my opinion regarding a certain decision that he needed to make related to the functional area of work that he managed. We talked for a while, and I gave him my opinion about what I would do if I were he. He thanked me and left our meeting. Not many days later I discovered that he had gone back to his people and told them that I was requiring him to make changes in his organization. That was never my intention as we spoke! I learned a valuable lesson that day. As a leader, never underestimate the power of what you say.

Jesus understood clearly the power of His words. It is interesting to observe in the Gospels the response of people to His words. As He taught, people noticed something different about His teaching style. They recognized that Jesus spoke with authority, unlike other religious teachers of the day (Mark 1:22). Something about the authority of Jesus' words attracted people to Him. His words also angered the religious leaders, creating envy among those who felt that He was becoming a threat to their religious system.

He knew what God the Father wanted Him to say and when He wanted Him to speak. To this day Christians read, teach, and preach the words of Jesus. They bring hope, comfort, and direction to our lives. His words are the very words of God. They bring light in our dark world.

The Words of a Kingdom-Focused Leader

The Bible warns us about losing control of our tongues. We read verses like: "For we all stumble in many ways. If anyone does not stumble in what he says, he is a mature man who also able to control his whole body" (James 3:2). Leaders easily forget to watch what we say and how we say things to others. There is an old Hebrew saying that "words are living things!" That is true. How many times have we lived to regret hurtful or careless words we have spoken to our family, spouse, or employees? We can never take back our words.

The kingdom-focused leader must be willing to submit to Jesus Christ as Jesus submitted to the Father. And we must be willing to say only what God directs us to say. As leaders we must watch our words and how we use them. It is displeasing to the Lord when His leaders are careless in their words. "I tell you that on the day of judgment people will have to account for every careless word they speak. For by your words you will be acquitted, and by your words you will be condemned" (Matt. 12:36–37).

The Bible calls us to let no unwholesome words come out of our mouths. "No rotten talk should come from your mouth, but only what is good for the building up of someone in need, in order to give grace to those who hear." (Eph. 4:29). Jesus said about the tongue, "It's not what goes into the mouth that defiles a man, but what comes out of the mouth, this defiles a man" (Matt. 15:11). He said also: "But let your word 'yes' be 'yes,' and your 'no' be 'no'" (Matt. 5:37).

Kingdom-focused leaders prayerfully consider what God wants them to say and when they should remain silent. One fruit of the Spirit is self-control (Gal. 5:23). Ask God to help you exercise restraint and to control your tongue so that everything you say is pleasing and acceptable to Him. Let me challenge you to pray before beginning each workday, asking the Lord to show you what to say and what not to say!

The psalmist said, "May the words of my mouth and the meditation of my heart be acceptable to You, O LORD" (Ps. 19:14). These words should be the prayer of every kingdom-focused leader. The leader's speech should be "gracious with salt," as Paul the apostle said (Col. 4:6). So today, pause and reflect. *Do my words honor the Lord? Are my words influencing others to have a stronger relationship with Jesus Christ? Will the words I say today help to advance the kingdom of God?*

Whether we are at home with our families, among friends, at church, or at our workplace, our words say more about what is within our hearts than anything else! If the kingdom of God is the reign of Jesus Christ within us, there will be a difference in our words.

Jesus Did Only the Works That the Father Wanted Him to Do

Jesus said, "These very works I am doing testify about Me that the Father has sent Me" (John 5:36). He also told the disciples, "My food is to do the will of Him who sent Me and to finish His work" (John 4:34). In three short years Jesus' work, His earthly ministry, changed the world forever.

Jesus' work pointed people to what God was doing in the world. As Jesus went about doing good, He healed the sick, cast out demons, and raised the dead. He called out a group of men who would be His leaders to extend His work when He left this world. The people were amazed by His works. "Then they were all amazed, so they began to argue with one another, saying, 'What is this? A new teaching with authority! He commands even the unclean spirits, and they obey Him.' His fame then spread throughout the entire vicinity of Galilee" (Mark 1:27). His work taught them that God was actively at work in the world. Jesus' earthly ministry was a demonstration of how God works in this world, transforming and reconciling broken people to Himself.

Jesus' greatest satisfaction, His *food* as He called it (John 4:34), was to accomplish the mission of God the Father in His life. His work was to die as the sacrifice for sin. He determined to finish the work God had given Him to do.

Jesus' every action focused on accomplishing the Father's will. He was constantly aware of God the Father's authority over His work. He spoke repeatedly of God sending Him—twenty-four times in the Gospel of John alone. His works glorified God and provided a new and living way to God.

Works of a Kingdom-Focused Leader

Jesus did only what God wanted Him to do. One of the most important issues that every kingdom leader must answer is, Why am I doing what I do? Or perhaps ask it in another way, Am I doing what God wants me to do with my life? Are you using your work to share the gospel? Does your work give you the opportunity to connect with people who otherwise would never have a Christian witness? How does your work contribute to the advancement of the kingdom of God?

Norman Miller, chairman of Interstate Batteries, understands the importance of including spirituality in the workplace.

Interstate's chairman is vocal about his faith and candid about the spiritual dimension of his company. This has drawn national attention. The March 13, 1995 cover of *U.S. News & World Report* shows Miller, Bible in hand, next to the headline "The Rise of the Christian Capitalists."

"A band of spirited—and spiritual—entrepreneurs is changing business, politics and religion in America," the article opens. It goes on to describe a day at Interstate. "The men have shown up for work an hour early—at 7 A.M. on a Monday—for their weekly, voluntary Bible study group. They are drivers and salesmen, younger fellows mostly, wearing the company-issued green-pinstriped shirts. The Bible study is conducted with the blessings of Interstate chairman Norman Miller, a born-again Christian who believes religion not only belongs in the workplace but is an essential part of business success. . . . 'I need to be faithful to Jesus 100 percent of the time,' declares Miller. '*And* that includes my business.'"[1]

It is not so much what you do but *why* you do it that really makes the difference. Many people derive value and a sense of self-esteem from their work. I remember a man who retired from his work but never found anything else to do. Soon he died. His friends said that after he quit working, he lost all hope. God designed us to work. But our work needs to glorify God and advance the kingdom. We must take the time to consider prayerfully why we are giving time and energy to the particular work we are currently doing.

I know a man who thought he had to quit his job in the computer industry because he believed God would be pleased with him only if he joined a church staff. After praying and seeking God's will, he recognized that God had given him the abilities and networks in the computer industry and that he could do more to advance kingdom work by staying in the computer world than he could by joining a church staff.

One CEO of an elder-care company said it like this: "I have tried to maintain a consistent approach to life, whether it was in school or in my jobs before Sunrise. As a Christian my faith is the foundation on which I make my decisions and form relationships. This came out strongly when I functioned as the chief operating officer at Sunrise, hiring people, training them, and setting expectations for them."[2] This particular leader has the right focus. He is using his work to further advance God's kingdom agenda in the world.

Jesus Went Only Where the Father Wanted Him to Go

Jesus Christ went only where God the Father sent Him. He always acted on the Father's directions and lived in total submission to His will. Jesus said, "For I have come down from heaven, not to do My will, but the will of Him who sent Me" (John 6:38). His single-minded passion and purpose was to accomplish the work God had given Him to do. Just hours before His crucifixion, Jesus cried out, "Not My will, but Yours, be done" (Luke 22:42).

Jesus lived in the awareness that He had been sent by the Father on a specific mission. His lived out His life to fulfill that purpose. He carefully selected the places where He would go. His decision to go through Samaria brought Him face-to-face with a Samaritan woman so He could offer her living water (John 4:3–15). But Jesus was always careful to be in the place where the Father had assigned Him to be. Soon after Jesus told His disciples about the events that would occur prior to His death and resurrection, Luke tells us: "And it came about, when the days were approaching for His ascension, that He resolutely set His face to go to Jerusalem" (Luke 9:51 NASB). He lived a life consumed with the single goal of fulfilling God the Father's mission for His life.

Thankfully we can read *this* book today as transformed people because Jesus finished the work that gave Him to do. Millions and millions of people since the first century have confessed that Jesus Christ is Lord of all!

The Location of a Kingdom-Focused Leader

Jesus was sent by God the Father. Do you have a sense of being sent as a leader to your current work assignment? Are you convinced that you are in the right place on a mission from God to do His work? In my life I have moved my family to a number of different states in order to be where I believed God wanted me to be. I have no regrets about following the Lord and going where He has led me. As a Christian leader, are you content where God has placed you?

I heard a Muslim on the news the other day say unashamedly that he works in order to further the cause of Islam! He lives in America and believes that God has sent him here for that purpose. How ironic that this man understands this concept, even though he does not serve the true God!

Soldiers who are deployed throughout the world today have no say about where their commanders send them. The same is true for those of us who serve as kingdom-focused leaders. We must accept our assigned place of responsibility. We can't be like Jonah who tried to run somewhere else. We must remember that our commander, the Lord Jesus, has strategically placed His leaders throughout the world in order to accomplish His kingdom agenda.

So where is the best place for a kingdom-focused leader to be? You have probably heard this expression before, but it is still true: the best place to be is in the center of God's will for your life.

Every kingdom-focused leader understands that, like Jesus, he has been given an assignment in order to achieve God's purposes. The kingdom of God is the reign of Jesus Christ in, through, and around us. As we experience the power of Christ's lordship in our lives, we must be willing to look around us and see how God is working in our midst!

The perspective of Bill Pollard, former CEO of Service-Master, is an example of the principles of saying, doing, and going only where the Lord wants us to be. Pollard writes:

> My one priority is seeking and serving the Lord I love. He has called me to be a witness and a servant in all I do. At times this will have me intensely focused on business, and other times absorbed in my family, and still other times wrapped up in church or some other activity. The issue is not to put these responsibilities in juxtaposition so much as it is to ask: Is Christ in it? What does He want me to do?[3]

Kingdom-Focused Leaders Live Under Authority

Considering the reality that at this very moment the Lord Jesus Christ is the leader of the kingdom of God brings real assurance to a world that seems out of control. I know that Jesus is reigning in heaven in the highest seat of honor and that through my personal relationship with Him He now reigns in me. What incredible truths!

I heard a famous business leader make a speech. He was talking about the secret to being an effective leader. I was surprised when he said that the most effective leaders are those who understand how to be followers! He explained that leaders cannot lead others effectively if they have never had to follow a leader. Leaders learn how to submit to authority by being followers, and they can misuse their authority when they forget what it is like to submit to the leadership of another.

The kingdom-focused leader lives like Jesus, in submission to the Father as our leader! A Roman centurion requested that Jesus heal his sick servant. Jesus started to go with the man to his house to heal the servant. But the man stopped Him. "Lord," the centurion replied, "I am not worthy to have You come under my roof. But only say the word, and my servant will be cured. For I too am a man under authority, having soldiers under my command. I say to this one, 'Go!' and he goes; and to another 'Come!' and he comes; and to my slave, 'Do this!' and he does it" (Matt. 8:8–9).

Jesus was impressed by this man's faith: The Bible says: "Hearing this, Jesus was amazed and said to those following Him, 'I assure you: I have not found anyone in Israel with so great a faith!'" (Matt. 8:11). The soldier understood authority. He recognized Jesus' authority to heal his servant, but he also understood from the military viewpoint the importance of the chain of command. He told the soldiers under his own command to come and go. As kingdom-focused leaders we must understand that we serve under the command of Jesus Christ, the Lord of the kingdom of God.

Recently our country sent hundreds of thousands of our soldiers around the world to fight terrorism and political unrest. On the news it is always sad to watch soldiers say good-bye to their families, but they are under authority of the commanders who have given them their orders. They have no choice of where they will serve; they serve at the pleasure of their commanders.

The rule and reign of Jesus Christ starts in us and then works through us to accomplish God's purpose in this world all around us. This principle is important because we must learn to live in submission and obedience to the Lord of the kingdom and do what He has called us to do as leaders.

We must serve as kingdom-focused leaders in total submission to the Lord who has all authority in heaven and earth, while recognizing His absolute ownership of our lives, our families, and our careers, and living in unquestioned obedience to His purpose. This is what the soldier understood about authority and submission as he spoke to Jesus, when he said, "But only say the word. . . ."

Kingdom-focused leaders must submit to the Lord of the kingdom as Jesus submitted Himself to God the Father when He walked on this earth.

I have a friend who is a physician. He is a committed Christian, a deacon, and a Sunday school teacher. He loves practicing medicine. He is a leader in his community. He has sensed that God is calling him to surrender completely to Him as a leader in his field of work. At first he thought that he needed to quit his practice and serve as a foreign missionary. But after praying and asking God to show him His will, he has determined that God wants him to stay right where he is, in a town in rural Tennessee, to practice medicine. He could move to a larger town and make better money. Yet he believes that God wants him to work where he is because of the opportunities he has to advance the kingdom of God in that place.

My friend exemplifies the principles of total surrender, absolute ownership, and unquestioned obedience. He represents what it means to be a kingdom-focused leader under the Lord's authority. Thus, he says what he is told to say, does the work God tells him to do, and goes where the Lord directs.

4

The Three Dimensions of God's Kingdom

Bob and I finished our initial discussion about the kingdom-focused leader. He seemed satisfied by what he had heard. This was his summary: "So I think I understand now. First, as a Christian leader I need to have a clear understanding of the kingdom of God as a present reality. Next I must realize that Jesus Christ is the leader of the kingdom of God. Also, I must be willing to submit to His leadership over my life. Did I get it?"

I laughed and said, "You've got it! Bob, that is exactly what it means to have a kingdom focus as a leader."

Over lunch Bob continued to question me about the implications of the kingdom and its relationship to his leadership as a Christian businessman. He asked, "So how do I begin to apply these principles to my work? Do my Christian values really have any effect on my leadership? What are the important things I need to know and do if I am to become an effective kingdom-focused leader in the workplace?"

As Bob spoke, I could tell he was really serious about living as a kingdom-focused leader. I said to him, "Bob, the most effective leaders have something in common. They have the incredible ability to maintain a focus on what is most important and not be distracted by issues that might be urgent but are not the most significant. Jesus is the best example of this. Have you ever noticed as you read about Jesus that He was never in a rush? He never seemed distracted or confused about His priorities. He lived with a single focus on the kingdom of God and doing His Father's will."

Bob leaned forward at the table and responded, "That is so true. When I think about my business, the important things for me are my sales goals, the development of my staff, and, of course, my bottom line! I won't do very well as a businessman if I don't stay focused on those very important issues. The moment I get distracted by other things, no matter how urgent they may be, it seems that my business drifts and we lose our momentum. I become distracted, and I am not a very effective leader. So, back to my original question: What are the most important issues for a leader to focus his attention on?"

"Let me try to explain this by giving you another illustration from the physical world. The realities of our physical existence are set in place by the dimensions of height, depth, and width. You cannot live in the world without experiencing all three dimensions. They shape all of our experiences. Just as the natural world is a three-dimensional reality, the kingdom of God is three-dimensional.

"Think with me for a moment. The God who created the world in three dimensions—height, depth, and width—has designed His kingdom three-dimensionally: God is at work *in* us, *through* us, and *around* us. When a person comes to know Jesus Christ as Lord and Savior, the kingdom of God becomes a reality *in* his life. From that significant moment forward, the believer must continue to allow the Lord Jesus Christ complete rule and reign of his life." Paul said, "I no longer live, but Christ lives in me!" (Gal. 2:20). The kingdom of God begins within our spiritual life but is advanced *through* our actions. As we give our personal witness for Jesus Christ, we experience God working *through* us. God works through us as we lead others and minister to them in His name. As believers seek to advance the kingdom of God and begin to look *around* them for opportunities to advance the work of the kingdom, they determine where God is working and become involved with Him.

These three dimensions of kingdom reality become the primary focus of a kingdom-focused leader's life. Whatever else may require the attention of Christian leaders, it is crucial that they focus on these three dimensions of the kingdom in their leadership roles. These dimensions form the essence of kingdom focus.

You may be a leader who is distracted by your circumstances. You can't seem to get your focus. Much of your time is spent pursuing urgent issues, but you neglect the most important things in life. Or you might be a very successful Christian leader right now. You may be living by the standards of God's Word, seeking to glorify God through your life. However, without a clear focus on these three dimensions of kingdom reality, you will never be a kingdom-focused leader. You will miss the joy of understanding how your life and work are part of God's worldwide kingdom expansion plan. You will live with a feeling that something is missing in your life. Having the right focus on the three dimensions of the kingdom helps you to prioritize the issues you face as a leader. Your goals begin to align with God's agenda of the advancement of His kingdom.

Let's look at these dimensions in detail. As we will see, focusing on each of these dimensions truly revolutionizes the way we lead.

5

The Kingdom *in* You—
Responding to God's Call

Bob put down his coffee cup while we ate our lunch. He looked as if he had something on his mind. I asked, "Bob, so what are you thinking?" He replied, "I have never thought of God's kingdom as having three dimensions like the physical world, but it makes sense!"

I smiled and said, "As I have gotten older, I have started wearing glasses. It has always been a challenge to keep up with them. I remember that when I had my fortieth birthday, I told the doctor that I was having problems seeing. He looked into my eyes with his instruments, smiled, and said, 'Congratulations! You have turned forty!'"

"Not long ago I started wearing bifocal glasses. I have come to the point where I can't see anything up close or far away! When I first got these new glasses, I really had a hard time focusing. I had to look carefully at objects in order to focus my eyes because of the different strengths of the lenses."

As a kingdom-focused leader, learning to distinguish between the three dimensions of kingdom reality is very important. Just as I had to adjust my sight to my new glasses, the kingdom-focused leader must learn to focus on the three dimensions of the kingdom.

The first and most important dimension of kingdom reality is how the kingdom is experienced *in* the life of the leader. Don't overlook this principle. This is where the kingdom of God always begins.

Jesus told Nicodemus, a religious leader who was searching to discover more about Jesus' teachings, "Unless someone is born again, he cannot see the kingdom of God" (John 3:3). After we come to know Jesus Christ as Lord and Savior, we begin to experience life changes in attitudes and character. The kingdom of God begins in you when you make Jesus Christ Lord of your life.

Foster Friess is president of Friess Associates, Inc., an investment company in Jackson, Wyoming.

> Despite growing up in a Christian home, Friess didn't become a follower of Jesus Christ until challenged by a potential client to submit his will to God. "I had a high-level board meeting with myself," says Foster, "deciding who should be the chairman of my board. And I got down on my knees on an October day over twenty years ago and asked Jesus Christ to take control of my life. Accepting Him as Lord has made a profound difference."[1]

The kingdom-focused leader first experiences a change in character because of the work of the kingdom of God on the inside. God always works on us from the inside out. He first changes us inwardly; then the outward actions begin to change. His mission is to transform us to become like Jesus and to produce the fruit of the Spirit in us. Spiritual transformation is God's work within us to change us. When we first become Christians, God begins this work in us. "If anyone is in Christ, there is a new creation" (2 Cor. 5:17). In his book *Just Like Jesus,* Max Lucado says, "God loves you just the way you are, but he refuses to leave you that way. He wants you to be just like Jesus."[2] How can that be? How can this happen?

Spiritual transformation, daily becoming more and more like Jesus, is a God thing. It is something that God does in you. You can't make it happen. You can't set goals and create a plan to do this yourself. So how does God do this work of radically changing you? The Holy Spirit does it through a personal, intimate relationship with you in which He transforms your innermost being. This relationship is characterized by love, trust, and obedience. There is no spiritual transformation apart from a relationship with God. The major agents that God uses to transform believers are:

- Scripture
- Family
- The Church
- Circumstances of Life
- Spiritual Exercises for Godliness
- God's Discipline

As a kingdom-focused leader you should be progressively becoming more like Jesus as God works in you. The intensity of your relationship with Jesus will determine your spiritual growth. Such growth develops from obedience with the appropriate motive—love of God and trust in Him.

Your inner transformation will be evident to the people in your life: spouse, children, fellow workers, employees, customers, competitors. Others will notice that you live in harmony with God's Word, have a biblical worldview, fellowship with other believers, and are concerned about those you encounter who do not yet believe in Jesus. The fruit of the Spirit—love, joy, peace, patience, kindness, goodness, faith, gentleness, and self-control (Gal. 5:22–23)—will be visible expressions of how you deal with the complexities of life. Your character will be transformed as you respond to the demands and events of life as Jesus responded.

God's Call

God continues His work in you with the call to leadership. When a speaker uses the phrase "God's calling," leaders often tune out, assuming he is talking to someone else. In our church culture, God's calling is understood as something that only happens to pastors, ministers, and missionaries. Gene Wilkes, in his book *My Identity in Christ*, gives a good explanation of this misunderstanding:

> We have confused the biblical idea of *calling* with *career* in today's church. Let me demonstrate. Four people stand in front of you—a nurse, a public school teacher, a lawyer and a pastor. Based on your experiences, which one would you most likely choose as the one who had answered God's call in his or her life?

If you chose the pastor, as I did, you would probably be in agreement with most Christians. We assume that someone who gave up a career in the marketplace to preach and lead people in the church surely had followed God's call, while the others pursued their own desires. Certainly a pastor is living his life in commitment to what God wants him to do. It's easy to think the nurse, teacher and lawyer aren't quite as "called" as the preacher, or they, too, would be out preaching or on the mission field.

Many Christians tend to think that unless you have forsaken all to live on a foreign mission field or in a parsonage, you have not really accepted God's call for your life. We have mistaken call for career. God's call affects every aspect of our lives. When you say yes to God, it does not change who signs your paycheck. It changes what you do with who you are, what you make, and what you have. . . .

[In the biblical record], when God called a person it had nothing to do with whether he was a warrior, shepherd, farmer, tax collector, or Pharisee. God's call was never about vocational counseling. It was always about joining Him in what He was doing to redeem His creation. I also never find pastor or prophet in Scripture as categories for jobs at a job fair. Career is our designation for a job path. Career is not in the vocabulary of the Bible.

Calling, on the other hand, is in the Bible. Regardless of one's job, God called men and women to be instruments of His work on earth. God often used the skills the person had learned to enhance that call, but the call, not the career, was God's interest. . . .

[Os] Guinness writes, "Calling is the truth that God calls us to himself so decisively that everything we are, everything we do, and everything we have is invested with a special devotion, dynamism, and direction lived out as a response to his summons and service."[3]. . .

God's call is so decisive in a person's life that it affects every aspect of his life. All we are, all we do, and all we have are the God-given resources to do what God had called us to do. God's call is not about where we send our resumé, but about changing our direction and purpose in life—no matter where we work! Simply put, a Christian's life is a gracious response to God's call to follow.[4]

Mike and Debi Rogers, in their book *The Kingdom Agenda: Experiencing God in Your Workplace,* speak to the same issue of how we have segmented the secular and sacred. We are guilty of compartmentalizing God's activity to a particular area of our life—the church. We tend to categorize the world in which we live as having secular and sacred parts. The Rogers say:

We even promote the idea that only a select group of individuals are truly about "the Father's business." In fact, many believe that unless a person is a preacher, a church or denominational worker, or a missionary, then one is not "in the ministry." It is beyond the scope of our traditional thinking to believe that God assigns or calls a person to a position such as bricklayer, traffic officer, file clerk, politician, farmer, accountant, scientist, writer, telephone operator, or physical therapist! We may think God is not involved in these jobs. We call them "secular" and therefore consider them insignificant to God. But they are important to God! Why? Because the kingdom of God does not stop at the doorway of the church building! The sovereign kingdom of God extends to the office, the factory, the classroom, the state house, the operating room, the cafeteria, the lab, and the boardroom.[5]

God's Call to Leaders

The Bible reassures leaders of their *calling to* leadership. Leaders often wonder if they're up to the task ahead of them; they wonder if they're really worthy of the call to lead. The Bible affirms that "we know that all things work together for the good of those who love God: those who are called according to His purpose" (Rom. 8:28). This means that every call to leadership comes from God and is to advance His kingdom on earth. Every call to lead is also a call to kingdom leadership. The kingdom-focused leader discovers that as the kingdom of God begins to take control of the leader's life from the inside, there comes a clear, distinct calling from God. God's call to leadership starts in our hearts and minds as we spend time with Him in prayer.

God's call to leadership is real, and it is personal; He has a personal encounter with those whom He has chosen and called to service. Regardless of our qualifications, no one is worthy of such a calling. The process is a mystery beyond our understanding. Yet when this incredible event occurs, we begin the journey as kingdom-focused leaders. The Bible is filled with reassuring examples of God's call to leadership. For example:

> Brothers, consider your calling: not many are wise from a human perspective, not many powerful, not many of noble birth. Instead, God has chosen the world's foolish things to shame the wise, and God has chosen the world's weak things

to shame the strong. God has chosen the world's insignificant and despised things—the things viewed as nothing—so He might bring to nothing the things that are viewed as something, so that no one can boast in His presence (1 Cor. 1:26–29).

I have a physician friend named Bryan. He believes that God has called him to practice medicine. He feels strongly that God wants him doing the work he is doing in a small town in Middle Tennessee. Bryan exemplifies the power of calling and the work of the kingdom on the inside of a man's life.

How is anybody supposed to be a leader? How do they know they're up to the task? How and where can they acquire the attributes and self-confidence they need? The Bible assures us that God lifts up leaders and then equips them to handle their responsibilities. It's not a role you or I can prepare for on our own, but we can rest in the knowledge that God will give us the skills we need and reaffirm our call throughout the time we are leaders.

Kingdom-focused leaders called by God today join the ranks of Abraham, Moses, Daniel, the disciples, Paul, and others whom God has specially selected and equipped. Every kingdom-focused leader is unique and comes to fulfill a specific purpose. Christ is the source of power and strength for all God's leaders.

Understanding God's Call

God's call should be etched on our hearts and lives. It is the touchstone for all that is to come in the life of a

Christian. His call is neither random nor arbitrary. He calls us "according to His purpose" (Rom. 8:28), and His call keeps kingdom-focused leaders secure in knowing they were called by and for Him.

In whatever they do, leaders become witnesses for Christ. To the extent that they model biblical standards of behavior and ways of treating others, they reach out to bring new people into the kingdom of God. Whether the witness is spoken or given by example, godly leaders are in a position to share their faith.

God's call to leadership is also a call to serve Him and serve others. Jesus modeled the servant leadership style. He is our example. Jesus said, "For even the Son of Man did not come to be served, but to serve, and to give His life—a ransom for many" (Mark 10:45). Jesus demonstrated servant leadership when He washed the feet of His disciples on the night before He was crucified. After doing this He said to them:

> "Do you know what I have done for you? You call Me Teacher and Lord. This is well said, for I am. So if I, your Lord and Teacher, have washed your feet, you also ought to wash one another's feet. For I have given you an example that you also should do just as I have done for you. I assure you: A slave is not greater than his master, and a messenger is not greater than the one who sent him. If you know these things, you are blessed if you do them" (John 13:12–17).

There's an old saying that "it's lonely at the top." God doesn't call leaders to serve alone. His call to service is a call to accompany Him on His mission in the world. Jesus assures us, "And remember, I am with you always, to the end of the age" (Matt. 28:20).

Leadership often requires sacrifice. But just as we look to Jesus for an example of great leadership, we also look to Him to see the costs involved. Peter wrote, "For you were called to this, because Christ also suffered for you, leaving you an example, that you should follow His steps" (1 Pet. 2:21).

Suffering and sacrifice are unpopular, even among Christians. But the fact is that God's call to kingdom-focused leadership is a call to self-denial and, when necessary, suffering. As Jesus made clear, "If anyone wants to come with Me, he must deny himself, take up his cross daily, and follow Me" (Luke 9:23). Answering God's call to be a kingdom-focused leader means denying ourselves and being willing to suffer for His sake.

Leadership assures a measure of suffering, but with the pressure of suffering comes the promise of God's presence and provision. "My goal is to know Him and the power of His resurrection and the fellowship of His sufferings, being conformed to His death" (Phil. 3:10). God calls us to join Him in fellowship and to go with Him in service, knowing that His call to leadership includes a call to suffering.

When Jesus called His first followers, they followed Him as their Lord. Their jobs—fishermen, tax collector, political operatives—became the means to an end. They used their vocations to support their call to follow Jesus Christ. The same principle applies to every kingdom-focused leader today.

Jesus' Response to God's Call

Of all the great leaders who have ever lived, no one better illustrates the reality of God's call than Jesus Himself. His life perfectly models unconditional response to God's call.

Like Jesus, kingdom leaders rejoice to do God's will. They are constantly aware of being commissioned by the Lord to spread His gospel message in addition to whatever else their leadership position involves.

Jesus modeled His leadership actions after those of God the Father, praying to Him, "Just as You sent Me into the world, I also have sent them into the world" (John 17:18). We in turn look to Jesus as our model, then pass His teaching on by our words and actions to those who follow us.

God's Calling to Kingdom Leaders

Successful leaders focus on Jesus Christ, who represents the essence of leadership. His life defines perfect leadership in word and deed. Kingdom-focused leaders serve the risen leader of the kingdom of God, Jesus Christ. Let's look at some noteworthy principles of the call of God and a life of kingdom-focused leadership.

- *Kingdom-focused leaders represent God in all they do.* Jesus modeled this principle perfectly, speaking only when the Father instructed Him to speak. Leaders should remain faithful to their Christian witness in all they do. Unfortunately, leaders sometimes veer off the Christian path. And when they lose the moral foundation their credibility is built on, they lose their ability to lead. Kingdom leaders must evaluate their words and deeds by what God would have them say and do.

- *Kingdom-focused leaders are to do God's work and none other.* Jesus performed the works of God with directness and clarity of purpose. Today's leaders are busier and more distracted than ever, always having to do more with fewer resources. Busyness, however, is no excuse for failing to do the Lord's work. Leaders must be attuned to what God would have them do and devote whatever energy is necessary to doing it.

- *Kingdom-focused leaders must serve willingly wherever the Lord assigns them.* Jesus was never anxious about where the Father sent Him. Kingdom leaders are to be content and happy in the places where God has assigned them. The Lord chooses where His leaders serve. This divine directive reassures leaders as they discover their places of service. Leaders who understand this principle are not jealous or resentful of other leaders, not miffed at being passed over for promotion, not upset if their assignment isn't as high-profile as someone else's. God directs all His leaders according to His perfect plan for their places of service to Him.

- *Kingdom-focused leaders must be obedient to God's calling.* Nothing better describes Christ's response to the Father's call than obedience, even obedience to the point of death on the cross. When the Lord sends a leader to a place of service, that leader has a specific task to accomplish. The kingdom leader makes it his life goal to obey the Lord and complete that work.

- ***Kingdom-focused leaders are confident God will equip them for leadership.*** God selects His leaders and gives them ministry gifts to accomplish His purposes. When Peter and John were arrested for their ministry in Jerusalem, they preached with authority before the same rulers who had crucified Christ. God gave the two disciples their courage and frankness. The rulers' response to Peter underscores this truth: "Observing the boldness of Peter and John and realizing them to be uneducated and untrained men, they were amazed and knew that they had been with Jesus" (Acts 4:13). These two fishermen obviously lacked formal training and skills, but just as obviously, God called and gifted them to be compelling witnesses for him. God will never call you to leadership without gifting you for the task.

6

The Kingdom *in* You— Developing Christlike Character

As we sat at lunch, Bob and I continued to talk about the leader's focus on the kingdom. Bob said, "What a difference this concept could have made in the life of those corporate leaders who have just destroyed their companies because they lacked character."

I agreed with Bob, "You have to wonder what they were thinking. It is amazing how people can flip a switch and forget everything they know about honesty and integrity."

Recently the corporate and financial world has been rocked by the unscrupulous dealings of major executives in various industries who did not tell the truth about stock values. These overrated stocks created a false rise in value. Just as these leaders were about to be discovered, they cashed in their stocks for enormous returns. Their unethical actions left others to experience the devastating loss of their investments.

The biggest bankruptcies in history occurred. Huge companies employing tens of thousands of people have disappeared, and millions of creditors and stockholders have suffered life-changing financial losses. This is the result of a small, exclusive group of rich and talented men and women who wanted to be even richer, even if it meant deceiving, lying, and breaking the law.

Now these rich, talented people face financial ruin, felony charges, and the prospect of years in prison, all because greed and the obsession for wealth consumed their lives. How different things might have been for them had they maintained a focus on their inner spiritual development instead of being consumed by "the love of money," which Paul said "is a root of all kinds of evil," adding that "by craving it, some have wandered away from the faith and pierced themselves with many pains" (1 Tim. 6:10).

"Character is what we do when no one is looking!"[1] That is how Bill Hybels describes character in his book *Who You Are When No One's Looking.* A kingdom-focused leader experiences the kingdom of God first on the inside by developing his or her spiritual life. God works to grow and shape Christlike character within the leader before He ever uses the leader for His kingdom's cause.

In a survey of leadership qualities, the characteristic most frequently mentioned—the characteristic considered most essential in a great leader—is credibility. The word comes from the Latin word *credo,* which means "I believe." Before anything else, a leader has to be believable. Credibility demands honesty and integrity, and without them leadership is impossible. The four characteristics that determine credibility are being honest, forward-looking, inspiring, and competent.[2]

While credibility results from consistency and honesty, it also preserves those characteristics and keeps them alive. The result is a circle of strength and affirmation that can sustain a leader throughout his life. That's a fortunate situation, because credibility must be renewed constantly. A leader can't achieve credibility at one point and then kick back and assume he has it forever. Men and women who lead have to reaffirm their credibility continually in order for it to be maintained.

Though credibility can be shattered in an instant, it is earned over time. Very seldom is there the opportunity to make some dramatic gesture that proves your credibility as a leader and makes others loyal to you. Most of the time the relationship builds modestly over time in layers. Keeping promises, leading by example, and listening and responding to the concerns of others gradually produces loyal, dedicated, and productive followers.

The work of the leader is to lead and inspire followers, but without character and the work of God on the inside, there is little hope for the leader to lead with credibility. Recently a vice president of sales faced a dilemma: as a Christian, was he to live for the Lord or the job? He was asked to lie about sales figures for the annual report. He told the boss no. He was fired for his unwillingness to cook the books and for what his boss called insubordination. He didn't make the news, but because of God's work of changing his nature from the inside, he left the company with integrity, with his character and credibility intact.

Our contemporary culture is characterized by moral relativism. It tends to shy away from the idea of any standard set of values as too old-fashioned or judgmental. When it comes to judging a leader, however, those old values suddenly become a lot more popular. The simple fact is that if there are no generally recognized standards of credibility, how can anybody decide whether anybody else is credible? It's impossible.

The only reliable source of behavioral absolutes is the Bible because it's the only reference we have based on the inerrant Word of God rather than the subjective views of man. There is no source that defines credibility as clearly as biblical teaching. And so, if character is the most essential component of leadership, the Bible is the most essential reference for a true understanding of the unchanging and all-encompassing nature of character. Even those who put another name on biblical absolutes will recognize their origin if they take the time to thumb through the Scriptures.

Don "Bubba" Cathy, senior vice president of Chick-fil-A, Inc., makes a case for the Bible as relevant in the business world. "The Bible is a great business tool . . . because the principles it teaches don't change. Technology and marketing dynamics change almost daily, and you have to keep up with them. God God's wisdom on how to treat people doesn't change."[3]

Zig Ziglar says: "Now just in case you're not quite as enthusiastic as I am about the value of biblical advice, . . .

I encourage you to remember this. According to the April 28, 1986, issue of *Fortune* magazine, 91 percent of the CEOs of Fortune 500 companies apparently learned their values, ethics and morals from the same source—the Bible and the church. At least they claimed affiliation with a Catholic or Protestant church or Jewish synagogue. (Less than 7 percent said they had no religion.)[4]

To anyone looking for the perfect example of a leader with credibility, Jesus Christ is the obvious and natural choice. His character is peerless and flawless, perfect in every way, faultless, authentic, and consistent. Jesus Christ is the perfect model for a kingdom-focused leader to follow. What about Jesus' character will benefit a bank president, a corporate executive, a college dean, a public official, or a project manager? The same characteristics of a balanced and upright life that we see in His life make for inspiring and successful leaders in the business world.

Because of the work of the Holy Spirit in us, we gain credibility. Credibility is the fruit of character. Character comes as God matures us through trials and tribulations in life. Kingdom-focused leaders grow in Christlike character through trials and the tests of life. Trouble builds character. Adversity is one of God's pathways to character development and spiritual vitality.

Abraham Lincoln once said, "Nearly all men can stand adversity, but if you want to test a man's character, give him power." Jesus built His leadership on the solid foundation of character that was tested and proven in the fires of real-life encounters. He obeyed God's call without hesitation and faced every difficulty as an authentic human being.

A Balanced Life

A doctor friend told me that the greatest single cause of sickness and depression in his patients is the lack of balance in their lives. He said most people spend very little time thinking about their inner spiritual life. They are more concerned with their outward appearance than their inner spiritual development.

The Bible tells us that in His youth, Jesus "increased in wisdom and stature, and in favor with God and with people" (Luke 2:52), suggesting that Christ's character revealed itself as He grew older. Jesus' balanced personal growth sets the pattern for all kingdom-focused leaders. Several characteristics revealed in Scripture touch on that balance.

- *Personal Holiness.* The trials Jesus endured confirmed His character. Even in the face of a hostile, sinful world, He remained free from sin. Such unblemished conduct could only come from flawless character. As Hebrews 7:26 proclaims, Christ is "holy, innocent, undefiled, separated from sinners, and exalted above the heavens." The pressures that kingdom leaders endure in a hostile world forge their character, test and mature their resolve. God sends them into that world, and He will protect them from it.

- *Resistance to Sin.* Even though He was the Son of God, Jesus experienced the temptation of sin. "We do not have a high priest who is unable to sympathize with our weaknesses," says Hebrews 4:15, "but One who has been tested in every way as we are, yet

63

without sin." Jesus experienced the strain of temptation all leaders endure. Every temptation we face, He
experienced as well. He overcame every temptation
that came His way, and His victory enables us to tri-
umph over sin as well: "For since He Himself was
tested and has suffered, He is able to help those who
are tested" (Heb. 2:18).

- *Faithfulness.* Jesus "was faithful to the One who
appointed Him" (Heb. 3:2). Christ demonstrated His
faithfulness by carrying out God's will regardless of
the consequences. Such faithfulness is essential for
kingdom leaders.

- *Obedience.* Perfect though He was, and without sin,
Jesus suffered a terrible death on the cross, made all
the more painful by the fact that He died in His per-
fection to give eternal life to a world of sinners.
"Though a Son, He learned obedience through what
He suffered. After he was perfected, He became the
source of eternal salvation to all who obey Him"
(Heb. 5:8–9). His character was shaped and molded
by His suffering. Kingdom-focused leaders soon
learn that faithful obedience to God brings suffering
to them as well, but such suffering is the crucible in
which their character is refined as they are prepared
for kingdom service.

- *Self-Sacrifice.* Of all the terms that best describe
Jesus' character, *self-sacrifice* is the superlative one.
Christ, the Lord of glory, put aside all the comforts of
heaven, all His privileges, all His splendor, to come

and give His life for the sins of the world. As the apostle Paul wrote, Jesus "made himself nothing, taking the very nature of a servant" (Phil. 2:7 NIV). The Lord of all sacrificed His all to do the work of God the Father. Such a level of self-sacrifice reveals Jesus' unsurpassed, God-given character and establishes God's pattern for all kingdom leaders.

- *Humility.* C. S. Lewis calls pride "the great sin" because without pride, other sins would have a much harder time taking root. Jesus "humbled Himself by becoming obedient to the point of death—even to death on a cross" (Phil. 2:8). He was the Son of God, who learned obedience from His earthly suffering, freely sacrificing His glory, honor, and authority to fulfill His God-ordained mission. Leaders will discover and develop the character required for kingdom leadership only when they discover and model the humility of Christ the king.

- *Christian Forbearance.* Some people think Christians are exempt from suffering, trials, and adversity, but Jesus' life reveals the error of that line of reasoning. The Bible tells us that "all those who want to live a godly life in Christ Jesus will be persecuted" (2 Tim. 3:12). Often, the more faithfully leaders follow kingdom principles, the more their troubles increase. True Christian leaders endure the result and rejoice in their identification with Christ, who warned that "if the world hates you, understand that it hated Me before it hated you" (John 15:18).

Kingdom-focused leaders can't expect to be treated any better than Christ Himself. Paul reminds us that as long as there are Christians in the world, God will develop their character through "afflictions, because we know that affliction produces endurance, endurance produces proven character, and proven character produces hope" (Rom.5:3–4). In spite of the world's hate, Jesus demonstrated character. He expects no less from kingdom leaders.

Experience shows us that successful leaders are contented leaders. Contentment is the ability to be at peace regardless of the circumstances. Paul declared, "But godliness with contentment is a great gain. For we brought nothing into the world, and we can take nothing out" (1 Tim. 6:6–7). Paul learned to be content no matter what his circumstances, from the extremes of having nothing to having an abundance of resources available to him (Phil. 4:9–13).

Larry Burkett put together a series of Bible studies entitled *How Much Is Enough?* Leaders might ask themselves that question: How much is enough?

Does discontent lure leaders into the temptations of materialism. As Paul cautioned Timothy in 1 Timothy 6:8, we should all be content with food and clothing—the basics of life. "But those who want to be rich fall into temptation, a trap, and many foolish and harmful desires, which plunge people into ruin and destruction" (1 Tim. 6:9). Every kingdom-focused leader faces the same challenge regardless of the kind of organization he or she leads. Kingdom-focused leaders lead from Christlike character, not from selfishness or personal greed.

Paul's Leadership List

The qualifications for leadership that Paul listed in a letter to his young assistant Timothy are qualifications any leader would do well to apply to his leadership role. Though these character qualities define what is expected of pastor leaders, the list is also helpful for other kingdom leaders. Read through the list and evaluate your own leadership character. Now, as in Timothy's day, these qualities form a foundation of honesty and accountability that supports great leaders in any field:

> This saying is trustworthy: "If anyone aspires to be an overseer [leader], he desires a noble work." An overseer, therefore, must be above reproach, the husband of one wife, self-controlled, sensible, respectable, hospitable, an able teacher, not addicted to wine, not a bully but gentle, not quarrelsome, not greedy—one who manages his own household competently, having his children under control with all dignity. (If anyone does not know how to manage his own household, how will he take care of God's church?) He must not be a new convert, or he might become conceited and fall into the condemnation of the Devil. Furthermore, he must have a good reputation among outsiders, so that he does not fall into disgrace and the Devil's trap (1 Tim. 3:1–7).

Breaking down this valuable and detailed listing, we see that Paul's leadership qualifications are not based on skills but on character. The Greek work for "character" is *dokimā,* which can be translated "the quality of being approved" or "genuine, without alloy." According to guidelines laid down by a disciple of the most successful leader who ever lived, Jesus Christ, genuineness and affirmation in the eyes of those being led are more important leadership characteristics than negotiating skills, accounting expertise, resource management ability, or any of those other abilities we're so quick to judge leaders on. Don't miss the point: kingdom-focused leaders lead out of character; their skills and gifts supplement the inward integrity of a life lived for God and the priorities of the kingdom.

Let's take a closer look at the list. Paul says church leaders should be:

- *Aspiring to Lead.* Desire to lead is not a selfish ambition but a genuine conviction of God's calling.
- *Above Reproach.* Leaders must not have hidden personal agendas. Their characters and lives must be beyond suspicion. They are to live so responsibly that no one can bring any legitimate charge against them.
- *Faithful to Their Spouses.* God's standard for marriage is that every man and woman be faithful to his or her spouse. Faithfulness in marriage indicates faithfulness in all aspects of a person's life. A kingdom leader is a model of marital commitment.
- *Self-Controlled.* Leaders exhibit temperance and restraint in all aspects of life. Demonstrating physical, spiritual, emotional, and social balance show an effective self-control in mind, body, and spirit.
- *Respectable.* Leaders are sensible, serious, mentally and emotionally stable, unbiased in judgment, prudent, and discerning. Their lives are dignified and orderly, revealing an inner solidity that is a worthy example to others.

- *Hospitable.* God's leaders show hospitality, not only to family, friends, and colleagues but also to outsiders, strangers, and even adversaries.
- *Teachers.* Teaching is an essential gift of leaders. They must convey what they know, explain what they expect, and communicate clearly on every level. They must teach in the power of God's truth at all times.
- *Straight and Sober.* Kingdom leaders are not to fall under the control of alcohol or other drugs. The Greek word here for "not addicted" suggests freedom from dependency on any type of addictive substance.
- *Gentle.* True leaders don't settle disputes with blows, whether physical or verbal. They are not quick-tempered and do not browbeat people in order to win their case. Kingdom leaders are flexible and approachable, yielding graciously when they are wrong and refusing to manipulate others. They embrace Jesus as their model of gentleness.
- *Agreeable.* Christlike leaders are not quarrelsome or argumentative. They don't verbally attack others, nor do they waste their time on useless debates or wars of words.
- *Not Greedy.* Countless leaders have fallen because, no matter how much money they had, they craved more. God's leaders do not overemphasize wealth and do not covet the wealth of their peers or anybody else. Kingdom leaders are content with income and resources adequate to meet their needs.

Kingdom leadership requires sharing and giving, not a spirit of covetousness.

- *Good Household Managers.* The family is at the center of God's plan for the human race. Kingdom leaders' families must be models of what God intends the family to be. These leaders encourage their children to trust in and follow the Lord. Their children should be known for their obedience and exemplary behavior.

- *Experienced.* Leaders must be mature enough to handle the pitfalls and pressures of their task. Maturity has little to do with chronological age but comes from life experiences and the lessons they teach. The heavy responsibilities of leadership place immature people in positions where they are vulnerable to the dangers of pride, disappointment, and frustration. These feelings cause leaders to make hasty and careless decisions. Successful, seasoned kingdom leaders know the importance of growing and maturing in their development, and in their walk with the Lord.

- *Reputable Among Outsiders.* The credibility and effectiveness of any leader can be measured by how others, especially outsiders, respond to him. Their impressions help the leader's organization recognize and define his character and integrity.

Though this list from 1 Timothy 3 is not an exhaustive list, it is a healthy overview of essential character traits for kingdom-focused leaders. They are worth reviewing carefully and often by leaders, organizations, headhunters, boards of directors, and every other component involved in matching leaders to tasks and having a stake in the outcome. These qualities provide a measurement for leaders to use to evaluate their leadership within their organizations based on character and heart.

I know a Christian businessman who uses this list to evaluate what he calls his "leadership values" once a year to determine how he is progressing. As he works through the list, he grades himself on his growth in character year to year. He is focused on God's work *in* his life. As a result of the evaluation he makes yearly of his spiritual goals, he continues to mature spiritually and become the kind of kingdom leader he should be.

In our culture many Christian business leaders have compartmentalized their lives, separating the secular workplace from their Christian values. A kingdom-focused leader understands that it is essential to live God-honoring, Christ-centered, Bible-based values in every aspect of life, including the workplace.

Brad is a kingdom-focused leader in Kentucky who works as a corporate trainer for a Fortune 500 company. He is active in his church and community and committed to living his life in the world according to biblical standards. He was surprised to hear that Zack, the broker who handled his investment and retirement accounts, was involved in an adulterous affair with another employee and was in the process of divorcing his wife. Brad and Zack go to the same church and interact in social circles in the community.

Brad made an appointment with Zack and informed him that he was moving his accounts to another brokerage. Zack was stunned that Brad would do this and asked him why. Brad said, "Because you are involved in an affair and have left your wife and daughter." Zack explained that what was going on in his personal life did not affect his professional life, and he assured Brad that he could trust that his finances would be in good hands. Brad responded by saying, "If I can't trust you to be faithful to your wife, I certainly can't trust you with my money." For Brad, it was a matter of character. What would happen in our culture if kingdom-focused leaders lived by that kind of standard and expected other believers to be accountable to the same values?

Portraits of Leadership Character

Kingdom leaders are *teachers*. They are mentors—wise and trusted counselors to those who follow them. They help students establish standards of personal discipline and are patient in giving instruction. Teachers have the gift ability to absorb and process information, and they never tire of learning. Throughout their lives, they continue to learn from everyone and every circumstance they encounter as they prepare the next generation to lead.

A picture is worth a thousand words. Like points on the leadership compass, kingdom leaders can gain further insights into their roles by focusing on the rich analogies, the word pictures, the New Testament provides to enlighten and guide. In 2 Timothy 2:3–6, the apostle Paul presented three word pictures of kingdom leaders that illustrate different sets of character requirements.

Kingdom leaders are comparable to *soldiers*. As troops in the field suffer hardship, so do leaders on the figurative field of battle. Business is filled with war metaphors, and the parallels are significant. Soldiers are not overwhelmed by adversity because they expect and have planned how to meet it. Soldiers are focused and disciplined; they submit to authority going where assigned and doing as ordered. True leaders have the same resolve and resiliency whatever the nature of their job.

Kingdom leaders have much in common with *athletes*. They compete according to the rules, even though compliance makes winning harder. To win fairly under the authority of a judge or referee, athletes discipline themselves and train rigorously. Great leaders follow God's rules, knowing they will one day give an account to God for their calling to lead. A famous golfer was disqualified as the leader in a tournament because he neglected to take a penalty stroke on a hole. He didn't follow the rules. In 1 Corinthians 9:24–27, Paul uses this athlete metaphor and ends with why it is important to be disciplined so as not to be disqualified:

> Do you not know that the runners in a stadium all race, but only one receives the prize? Run in such a way that you may win. Now everyone who competes exercises self-control in everything. However, they do it to receive a perishable crown, but we an imperishable one. Therefore I do not run like one who runs aimlessly, or box like one who beats the air. Instead, I discipline my body and bring it under strict

control, so that after preaching to others, I myself will not be disqualified.

Kingdom leaders are like *farmers.* Successful farmers prepare well, plowing, planting, fertilizing, and caring for the crops as they grow. They work hard, knowing the requirements of their work day and night, summer and winter. Yet farmers are patient. They must wait for the rain, watch the rising and falling of the market, nurture the crop, and harvest in season. And they must seize the opportune moment, changing their plans quickly and confidently to respond to changing conditions in the weather, the markets, or other variables. Kingdom leaders also need to prepare, be patient, work hard, and remain flexible. A dear friend farmed over two thousand acres in Okalahoma for many years. I asked how he could keep farming. He replied, "It's the hope of the harvest that keeps me going from year to year."

This chapter has presented a kaleidoscopic view of biblical attributes of the kingdom leader's character. Character comes as a result of trials in the life of the leader. But kingdom leaders are never alone. They experience the power of God in their lives. As a result of salvation in Jesus Christ, God's call to leadership, and His work in the leader to develop character, the leader grows spiritually. This growth prepares the leader to be useful to God as "a special instrument, set apart, useful to the Master, prepared for every good work" (2 Tim. 2:21). This prepares you for the second dimension of kingdom reality, God's working *through* the kingdom-focused leader.

7

The Kingdom *Through* You

I never thought that God could ever use me if I wasn't a preacher," Bob replied. "I have always assumed that God worked through preachers but didn't really have a special job for me to do."

I said to Bob, "I will always remember, after I moved from the pastorate to a new leadership role, going into the conference room and looking at the frustration on the faces of the employees who were gathered around the meeting table. It was apparent that no one wanted to be there. People did not want to make eye contact with their peers, afraid that if they did it would confirm their own feelings of disgust.

"Finally the leader of the group came into the meeting. He had no idea that the atmosphere of the meeting was all about him. None of his people had any confidence in him. They did not believe he deserved his job. All thought that he had his position because of his relationship with the CEO. One employee said to me, 'My boss is clueless!'"

If you have ever worked for a leader who lacked ability to do his job, you may have felt like those employees. You know how frustrating it is.

I am convinced that leadership is a gift, not a skill. Leaders are born, not made. You can help a leader get better, but you can't make a follower who isn't born to lead into a leader. I often say, "You never have to tell leaders to lead. They do it naturally."

One of my friends who is a preacher says, "It doesn't matter what you do to a pig. Paint his nails. Put a bow on his head. Whenever he gets the chance, he will still get in the mud. A pig is a pig! It is his nature to get in the mud." Leaders lead whether they have a title or position in the organization.

One of the great discoveries for you as a kingdom-focused leader is to learn how God works *through* you. The truth revealed in Scripture is that you are His instrument to do His work in the world. God works through you to make a difference in the world as you function as salt and light. Your assignment is to point people to Jesus. He wants to work through you to impact the people in your sphere of influence for His kingdom.

Influence is a key concept in defining leadership. Mike Rogers captures the significance of influence in his article, "Church Members in the Marketplace: How to Develop Influential Leaders":

> If leadership could be described in one word, it would be *influence*. This word captures the essence of what a leader has that makes others want to follow. The world's idea of leadership describes this influence from a humanistic perspective built upon human sufficiency, human potential, and the limited resources of human nature. Leadership, according to the world's viewpoint, comes from:

- one's position of authority
- one's ability to do something to somebody
- one's ability to do something for somebody
- one's degree of honor or respect
- any combination of the above

While significant, these leadership resources are founded in human nature. They are man-centered and vulnerable to the flaws of human nature. Other qualities used to influence people are: the excitement of a cause, communication skills, political influence, physical beauty, natural charisma, financial resources, and intellectualism.[1]

The main difference between the world's perspective on leadership and a kingdom-focused leader is Jesus.

Examine the life of Christ, and try to apply the world's models of leadership in light of His life. You will discover a striking difference. . . . It is a leadership not dependent upon position in life, financial or social well-being, or political connections. . . .

It is God in Christ who transforms the world. It is Christ in you who will lead others into the kingdom of God. This kind of leadership comes from one's relationship with Almighty God.

Jesus told His disciples, "If anyone loves me, he will obey my teaching. My Father will love him, and we will come to him and make our home with him" (John 14:23).[2]

The goal of kingdom-focused leadership is to cooperate with God. A kingdom-focused leader is a person whose influence is powered by the indwelling Christ.

The power and authority of God's presence should be what people encounter in us. I believe that the most influential people in this life are those through whom others can experience the presence and power of Almighty God.

[In the Sermon on the Mount, Jesus] answered the question that we ask over and over again: *What is God's will for my life?* He said, "You are the salt of the earth . . . you are the light of the world . . . let your light shine before men, that they may see your good deeds and praise your Father in heaven" (Matt. 5:13–14, 16).

In those few words He charted the course, wrote our earthly destiny, and clarified our purpose. We are to be people of influence—people under His influence. We are to be the most influential people on this earth! Glancing back at the beatitudes quickly reminds us that Christ's type of influence is not like the world's. Its source is not found in the potential of human nature. It is found in the power and presence of God. The most we can do is cooperate with God in such a way that we do not hinder His work. Yet, as I listen and observe the Christian landscape, I find that we often fail to call people to God's destiny for their lives in the arena of the workplace. Few really understand God's call for their lives, and few know the peace of truly being in His will. . . .

Surprisingly enough, He told His disciples: "Believe me when I say that I am in the Father and the Father is in me; or at least believe on the evidence of the miracles themselves. I tell you the truth, anyone who has faith in me will do what I have been doing. He will do even greater things than these" (John 14:11–12).

They will do even greater things than He did? How? Through their own strength and power? No, it would have to be a "God thing"! The answer is in our willingness to allow God to work [through] our lives. Jesus chose people who had no position of leadership and power to become people through whom God's power might be demonstrated. . . .

The focus is on becoming the church in the world. Therefore, the focus of my work is to allow God to work through me . . . so that others might be touched by God. I constantly remind myself that I cannot lead others where I have never been.[3]

Leadership Characteristics of Jesus

As we've already seen, the greatest leader of all time is Jesus. Jesus Christ's mission was to reveal the love and grace of God to all people. He continues to lead His people to advance the kingdom of God worldwide. Jesus is the model of one born to lead, with unique gifts and abilities that leaders recognize. Here are some of His leadership traits.

Kingdom Vision

Although He never traveled beyond Palestine, Jesus saw the world and what He would do in it through His disciples. Kingdom leaders must be gifted with kingdom vision. Otherwise, their concept of what they are supposed to do—and what they can do—will be far too small. Kingdom-focused leaders are captivated by the kingdom of God.

Jesus said to His disciples, "I assure you: The one who believes in Me will also do the works that I do. And he will do even greater works than these, because I am going to the Father" (John 14:12). Jesus saw from a kingdom perspective how through His disciples the kingdom of God would spread across the world.

Servant Ministry

As Jesus explained about Himself in Matthew 20:28: "The Son of Man did not come to be served, but to serve, and to give His life—a ransom for many." Kingdom leaders should follow His example of servant ministry. The picture of Jesus kneeling to wash His disciples' feet constantly reminds kingdom leaders of the importance of servant leadership.

Builder of Leaders

Jesus was the supreme leadership model and spent much of His time teaching and training leaders. He saw past their weaknesses into their hearts. He gave them a vision and drew out the best from them. Jesus called Peter and Andrew to follow Him. He promised to make them into fishers of men (Matt. 4:19). As He called disciples to learn from Him and follow His example, Jesus continues to call and enable leaders. The truth of this is evident in the growth of the church throughout the centuries.

Communicator

The Gospels present Jesus as the master preacher-teacher who astounded His listeners whenever He spoke. They had never before heard such powerful words. As Matthew reported after the Sermon on the Mount, "The crowds were astonished at His teaching. For He was teaching them like one who had authority, and not like their scribes" (Matt. 7:28–29).

Ten Ministry Gifts for Leaders

A Christian businessman asked, "So what is it that makes leaders so different?" I think the answer is giftedness. It is not enough to be born a leader. God gifts kingdom leaders to do their work. You must remember that God started His work *in* you when you were born again. But He also gifted you to do your work for Him.

God gives kingdom-focused leaders the gifts they need to accomplish the work He calls them to do, and He expects them to recognize, develop, and use those gifts. Those gifts are supernatural, bestowed by God's grace, and one day all kingdom leaders will answer to God for what they have done with them. Natural-born leaders have an innate ability to lead, but kingdom leaders are divinely gifted by God at salvation with spiritual gifts. These gifts enhance the leaders' ability to serve God at full capacity and for God's kingdom to be advanced *through* their lives.

The Epistles of Paul list at least ten ministry gifts that are given to believers in the church. Kingdom-focused leaders must identify and understand the gifts God has given them as well as discern the leadership gifts of other people. These ministry gifts are to be used wherever he is called to exercise leadership—in the church, in the community, or in the workplace.

Let's take a moment to review the list of gifts that are given to God's people. Remember, not every leader has all these gifts. Also, this is not an exhaustive list of gifts but rather a list to help us to think about the kind of gifts God has given us. These are given to us supernaturally by God to equip us to do the leadership work that God has called us to do.

1. Administration. "And God has placed these in the church: first apostles, second prophets, third teachers, next, miracles, then gifts of healing, helping, managing, various kinds of languages" (1 Cor. 12:28).

Capable administrators are goal oriented and objective oriented. They tend to have strong organizational skills and the ability to coordinate resources to accomplish tasks quickly. They are motivated by the prospect of getting the job done and typically derive great satisfaction from viewing the results of their accomplishments.

2. Exhortation. "According to the grace given to us, we have different gifts: If prophecy, use it according to the standard of faith; . . . if exhorting, in exhortation" (Rom. 12:6, 8).

Men and women gifted in exhortation have a special ability to encourage others by offering words of comfort, encouragement, and counsel in times of need. They are often willing to share their own past failures to help motivate and uplift others.

3. Giving. "We have different gifts: If prophecy, use it according to the standard of faith . . . giving, with generosity" (Rom. 12:6, 8).

Generous people give time, money, and advice cheerfully. They aren't blinded by the desire for riches and so have a healthier and better balanced outlook on their careers and their lives. They are usually wise investors and effective money managers. They want to give quietly without recognition and are encouraged and honored when they see that their gifts serve to benefit others. They see financial needs and opportunities that others may overlook.

4. Helps. "And God has placed these in the church: . . . gifts of . . . helping" (1 Cor. 12:28).

This refers to the leadership gift of meeting the personal needs of others. Leaders enjoy extending an offer of immediate help to relieve others of their burdens. This generosity is motivated more by a desire to provide assistance than by a desire to accomplish a task.

5. Hospitality. "Share with the saints in their needs; pursue hospitality" (Rom. 12:13).

The gift of hospitality—making guests feel comfortable and welcome under any circumstances—is the hallmark of a great leader. In business or at home, for corporate leaders or the most junior employees, kingdom leaders always provide a warm greeting and an inviting environment. Hospitality is one of the most fundamental and universal ways of showing care and respect.

6. Mercy. "We have different gifts: If prophecy, use it according to the standard of faith; . . . showing mercy, with cheerfulness" (Rom. 12:6, 8).

Leaders with this gift are compassionate, deriving joy from meeting the physical, spiritual, or emotional needs of people in distress. In fact, merciful leaders often attract other people in need of friendship and counsel based on deep communication and mutual commitment. They have the ability to draw out the feelings of others and are willing to be vulnerable. They look for solutions that avoid conflict and confrontation.

7. Prophecy. "According to the grace given to us, we have different gifts: If prophecy, use it according to the standard of faith" (Rom. 12:6).

Prophecy in this sense means *truth telling,* and these leaders have the ability to proclaim the truth without compromise. They have strong convictions and expect the truth from others. They need to express themselves in words, especially when it comes to right and wrong. Prophetic leaders may be quick to judge others and quick to express their opinions. They have a keen ability to discern the sincerity of others and may be painfully direct when correcting someone. They are persuasive in defining right and wrong and persistent in expressing their feelings about the need for change.

8. Service. "We have different gifts: If prophecy, use it according to the standard of faith; if service, in service" (Rom. 12:6–7).

Men and women who are service-oriented enjoy doing things that benefit others and meet practical needs. They may disregard their own personal health and comfort to serve others and have a hard time saying no when asked to help. They often have an affinity for clear details and, consequently, appreciate clear instructions. They enjoy the process of serving as much as the end result and derive satisfaction from being with others who also serve.

9. Shepherding. "And He personally gave some to be apostles, some prophets, some evangelists, some pastors and teachers" (Eph. 4:11).

Leaders protect those who follow them and accept ultimate responsibility for whatever happens as a result of their work. *Pastor* translates a Greek word meaning "shepherd." Leaders see guiding, encouraging, and nurturing their followers as a sacred, God-given responsibility. They are motivated by a desire to see those under them succeed.

10. Teaching. "We have different gifts: If prophecy, use it according to the standard of faith; . . . if teaching, in teaching" (Rom. 12:6–7).

Leaders want to share their knowledge and experience with others. They have the passion and the ability to research and present a true account of events in an organized, systematic fashion. They are alert to details and place great emphasis on accuracy. They believe teaching is a basic foundation for building future success.

Kingdom-focused leadership, we see once again, is the result of divine calling and empowerment, not just human ability. Kingdom leaders acknowledge this, recognize Jesus as the perfect example of leadership in every field, and live secure in the comfort of knowing Jesus has called them as He Himself was called. They learn that their skills and abilities have been given to them to advance the kingdom of God, not their own personal agendas or selfish ambitions. As kingdom-focused leaders grow in character and discover the giftedness by which God can work through their lives, they begin to look around them to see how they might be used to advance the kingdom of God.

Paul said it best: "not I but Christ in me" (Gal. 2:20). As a kingdom-focused leader, he understood that the second dimension of the kingdom is God working *through* the life of a believer equipped by the Holy Spirit to advance the cause of God's kingdom in the world.

Here are some key questions that have helped me to make the adjustments needed to become a kingdom-focused leader:

- How is God's presence in my life visible to those around me?
- What in my life is limiting God from influencing others through my life?
- In what ways is God's influence in my life impacting my:
  - → character?
  - → relationships?
  - → priorities?
  - → competence?
  - → self-image?
  - → vision?
- How is my relationship with God affecting my daily work life?
- Am I satisfied with the assignment God gave me, or am I always thinking of the next one?
- What aspects of my human nature dominate my decisions and behavior and undermine the sovereignty of God over my heart?
- If Jesus were given my assignment, how might He flesh it out?

- Am I willing to trust God with my agenda, life, future, and career?
- What is God showing me in my current circumstances that will improve my servant calling?[4]

8

The Kingdom *Around* You

W ow" Bob said, "You have really challenged me to consider how God can work through me as a leader in my
business. It is amazing that God has a place and purpose for
me and that He will work through me if I am willing to allow
Him to do it."

I replied, "You are getting it, Bob. There is one more
dimension for you to consider. God is at work in you as a
kingdom-focused leader, and He desires to work through
you. The next step is for God to open your spiritual eyes so
that you can see Him at work around you, so that you can
join Him in what He is already doing."

I'll never forget the first time I heard Henry Blackaby
describe how God is at work in the world. He was talking
with a group of leaders in a meeting about his teaching on
Experiencing God. One of the most exciting things he
described was the believer's responsibility to "watch to see
where God is working and join Him"![1]

Perhaps you, too, have been challenged by this truth. How
do you find where God is at work and join Him? This

question best describes what I want you to consider in the third dimension of the kingdom: God's work in the world around you. I often think about this responsibility as a leader. The kingdom-focused leader must discern God's kingdom work *around* him. Let me ask you this question: Are you aware of how God is working around you? Based on your answer, you will know how sensitive you are to the third dimension of kingdom reality. God's kingdom work is going on all around us, but we must have the spiritual sensitivity to see it.

I once had the opportunity to sail a forty-nine-foot yacht. It was the chance of a lifetime. A friend invited two of my colleagues and me to come to the British Virgin Islands to sail with him. It was a wonderful adventure. But while sailing, I learned a valuable lesson about focus.

We were sailing on some of the most beautiful water in the world. The trade winds were gently blowing, and the temperature was a perfect seventy-two degrees. But in order to sail the yacht, I had to maintain my focus. I had to keep my eye on the horizon and the island that was ahead of us, which was our destination. It was my responsibility to steer the yacht into the winds. Without wind the yacht loses its power to sail. I had to keep my eye on the wind directional gauge to ensure that I was tacking into the winds. I couldn't be distracted by the beautiful surroundings. I had to maintain a firm grip on the wheel and keep my focus on the horizon, the island, and the directional gauge.

The kingdom-focused leader must learn, while living in a world of distractions, the importance of being focused on

God's activity around him. It is easy to give in and become discouraged. Sometimes it seems that God is not at work in the world today or that God is losing the battle against evil and the devil. But the truth is that God continues to grow the kingdom, and the kingdom-focused leader learns to recognize that activity.

Jesus lived in full awareness of God's work in the world. He said, "My Father is still working, and I also am working. . . . The Son is not able to do anything on His own but only what He sees the Father doing. For whatever the Father does, these things the Son also does in the same way. For the Father loves the Son and shows Him everything He is doing, and He will show Him greater works than these so that you will be amazed" (John 5:17, 19–20). Jesus saw the work of God the Father in the world and joined Him. He invites us to do the same.

Kingdom-focused leaders look for opportunities to use their gifts and resources to help people become united with God through a personal relationship with Jesus Christ. Sometimes these opportunities come as they meet needs in the lives of others.

A Christian businesswoman saw the opportunity to help a group of military wives on a local army base whose husbands were on assignment in Iraq. She provided them with guidance, assisting them with their financial needs. Then she had the privilege of leading several of these women to faith in Jesus Christ. She saw God at work around her and joined Him in what He was doing. She was sensitive to the needs of others, and as a kingdom-focused leader, she sought to meet those needs.

Kingdom-focused leaders must look around as Jesus did for opportunities for the kingdom of God to be advanced. Jesus said to His disciples, "Open your eyes and look at the fields, for they are ready for harvest" (John 4:35). As a kingdom-focused leader, you see the fields around you waiting for you to step in and harvest.

The kingdom-focused leader understands that God is working the same way today as He did in Jesus' day. God is working to reconcile people to Himself. Listen to what Paul said: "Now everything is from God, who reconciled us to Himself through Christ and gave us the ministry of reconciliation: that is, in Christ, God was reconciling the world to Himself, not counting their trespasses against them, and He has committed the message of reconciliation to us" (2 Cor. 5:18–19).

When you sit down at your desk as a leader, have you identified the ways God is working around you? Have you committed yourself to joining Him? Are you willing to use your resources and your time advancing His work where He has placed you as a leader?

This is how Dan Cathy, executive vice president of Chick-fil-A, Inc., explains how his family lives out this principle. "The essence of why we're in business . . . is captured in our corporate purpose statement: 'To glorify God by being a faithful steward of what's entrusted to us and to have a positive influence on all who come in contact with Chick-fil-A.'"

This includes our corporate staff, our operators, our team members, and the public at large.[2]

> Bubba Cathy, Dan's brother and senior vice president speaks for the family when he says, "We believe we are stewards of all God has entrusted to us—not just of the financial resources we've accumulated, but most particularly of our people resources. One day we will have to give an account. The Bible says 'to whom much is given, from them much will be required.' The restaurant business is labor intensive, which gives us great opportunity to make a difference in the lives of our corporate staff, our operators, and the forty thousand people affiliated with Chick-fil-A restaurants. We want to help them reach their potential."[3]

John Wesley said, "I read the Bible to find out what I must do in the world. I read the newspaper to find out what God is doing in the world." John Wesley really had it right! As a kingdom-focused leader, the best way to learn where God is at work in the world is to take advantage of the many different media sources available today. We have at our disposal far more sources to discover what God is doing than John Wesley had when he spoke these words. Our sources are plentiful. They include TV news, magazines, newspaper, Internet articles, mission magazines, denominational papers, demographic studies, community newsletters, and business journals.

Why not try to use these media sources to identify God's activity in your area? Ask yourself questions such as these that focus on God's work in the world and not on your self-interest as you interact with various media:

1. How can God use this situation to further advance the kingdom of God?
2. What opportunities are available to me, based on this story, to use my resources and leadership influence to advance the kingdom of God?
3. Who are some other key Christian leaders who need to join me in developing a coalition to advance the kingdom around this particular issue.
4. How can I take what I have just learned and use it to advance God's work of salvation to people without Christ?

A very good friend of mine has started keeping a journal of things that he discovers from his reading of newspapers and other periodicals which he believes to be kingdom opportunities. As a result he has worked with several Christian agencies to develop projects that have advanced the work of the kingdom of God in his community.

Sometimes we forget how God has used advances in technology to advance His kingdom. Invention of the printing press made Bibles available for the first time to the common man in Germany. Soon the printing press provided Bibles for English readers.

Television and radio has been greatly used by God to advance the message of Jesus Christ and His saving grace around the world. Now we live in the Internet-connected world. Who would ever have dreamed that from our homes or offices we could connect with the world! We can help advance the kingdom agenda from our personal computers.

Some of you who are reading these pages are heavily involved in technology development. Have you ever stopped to think how your inventions can further advance the kingdom?

The kingdom-focused leader is passionate about the advancement of the kingdom. It is his first priority. The kingdom overshadows and consumes his thinking. Before any thought of personal gain or prosperity, the kingdom-focused leader carefully searches for opportunities for kingdom advancement.

Recently I attended a business seminar focused on leadership development in the business world. The training was very helpful to me personally. I learned many things I can use in my business work every day. However, I was convicted about something in the seminar that has stuck with me. The professor leading the seminar gave an impassioned speech about how he believes big corporate America could change the fortunes of the world. He believes that the world can become a better place if corporate America will do what it should do. He believes that because many businesses are now global, these companies, now larger in financial resources than some countries, should begin to lead the world in global advancement.

I have thought much about this professor's passion and true belief that these companies can make the world a better place. But I was convicted because I have not been in many meetings with Christian leaders and heard the same confident passion about how the kingdom of God can be advanced by a group of committed believers. God has placed believers in the world to provide what truly is the only real answer to the world's problems—having a personal relationship with Jesus Christ.

Kingdom-focused leaders learn to discern God's activity in the third dimension of kingdom reality—His work *around* them! The greatest adventure in life comes when we discover how God is working in our world and how we determine to become an agent for furthering the kingdom of God! Kingdom-focused leaders use every resource they have to discover and take advantage of the opportunities God brings them to advance His kingdom regardless of the costs! They look to see where God is working and join Him!

9

Living as a Kingdom-Focused Leader

As Bob and I finished our lunch, I could see that he was processing the implications of being a kingdom-focused leader. He said, "I really believe this will help me understand how God can use my life as a Christian business leader. It is exciting to know that God can work in me and through me. I need to begin to see how He is at work around me so I can join Him in His work. I think that is the dimension I was unaware of before our conversation. I believe this will help me to find the fulfillment I lacked as a leader, as I become a kingdom-focused leader."

When Bob and I finished our discussion that day, I left with a sense of satisfaction that I had done my part to encourage a fine Christian businessman that his life in the business world could be significant to God and the work of His kingdom. Bob's response to the time we spent encourages me. Since that day I have watched Bob put into practice the principles of living as a kingdom-focused leader. He no longer questions the value of his business work. He now understands that God has placed him where he is for a purpose. Bob is living in assurance that he can make a contribution to what God is doing in this world.

Paul expressed his personal satisfaction at the end of his life when he said, "I have finished the race, I have kept the faith" (2 Tim. 4:7). I hope that you share with me the desire to say those words at the end of your leadership assignment from the Lord. Most Christian leaders I have met have expressed in one way or another the desire to live their lives and contribute significantly to kingdom work in the world.

You can experience joy and satisfaction as you rivet your attention on the three dimensions of the kingdom and use your personal resources to advance the cause of Christ in your part of the world! When you do this, you come to understand what is really important to God. You reprioritize your life ambitions. Rather than focus on yourself, you have a cause to live for and to give yourself to that offers you ultimate meaning and purpose for the rest of your life! The most important thing to God is for lost people to have an eternity-changing experience through a personal relationship with Jesus Christ. When a kingdom-focused leader shares the gospel, he participates in heaven's highest priority!

God has designed His kingdom to be understood and experienced personally. The kingdom of God begins within you at conversion. God continues to work in you to develop your call and character. The kingdom is expressed through your life as you are salt and light in a lost world. It is at work all around you, but you must have spiritual eyes to discern

THE KINGDOM-FOCUSED LEADER

how you can join God in its global advancement. What a privilege to be called to be a kingdom leader. What a responsibility to live with a kingdom focus!

Kingdom-focused leaders leave a lasting legacy. I remember serving as interim pastor of a church after the retirement of a wonderfully gifted pastor. It was incredible to observe the lasting impact that this man had on the people in the congregation. They often spoke of his life and work among them. The plans and direction of the organization were set in motion by the work of this leader and continued after he left. He truly left a godly legacy for others to follow.

Of course no other leader has ever left such a legacy as Jesus. Over the past two thousand years, the kingdom of God has continued to grow to the point where hundreds of millions of people of every tribe and nation have come to know and serve Christ. His work goes forward undiminished—all this from a man who had a three-year ministry on the earth!

I enjoy reading adventure books, and one adventurer who has fascinated me is the British explorer Ernest Shackleton. Here was a leader who faced amazing obstacles and emerged victorious. In 1915, on his third trip to Antarctica, his ship, the *Endurance,* became trapped in the ice and eventually sank. As head of the expedition, he was responsible for the lives of twenty-seven other men. He kept them calm and hopeful until the giant ice floe they were drifting on reached a deserted island in the Weddell Sea. After setting up camp on the island, he took five men with him and went for help in a twenty-two-foot whaleboat they had saved before their ship sank. After sailing more than twelve hundred miles through the stormiest waters in the world, the six men were rescued, then led a search party back to the others they had left behind. The whole process took ten months, but Shackleton didn't lose a single man.

Recalling the adventure later, one member of the expedition said, "I have served with Scott, Shackleton, and Mawson, and have met Mamsen, Amundsen, Peary, Cook, and other explorers, and in my considered opinion, for all the best points of leadership, coolness in the face of danger, resource under difficulties, quickness in decisions, never-failing optimism, and the faculty of instilling the same into others, remarkable genius for organization, consideration for those under him, and obliteration of self, the palm must be given to Shackleton, a hero and a gentleman in very truth."

Recently I went to an IMAX theatre to see a presentation of the heroic journey of Shackleton, *Shackleton's Antarctic Adventure.* It was spectacular! The score and the story were overwhelming as we thought about Shackleton's courageous, fearless leadership. As we entered the theater, we were given 3-D glasses. I put them on when I sat down, and as the movie began, I struggled to focus my vision. But after several minutes I was able to experience the show in three dimensions!

My hope is that you will begin to see the work of the kingdom of God in 3-D. Nothing is more important than living with a three-dimensional focus on the kingdom of God for leaders who seek to become all that God wants them to be and who desire to use their leadership, gifts, resources, and position to advance the kingdom of God. This focus requires discipline and practice. But once you begin to focus on the kingdom *in* you, at work *through* and *around* you, there comes an excitement and fulfillment like no other.

For over twenty years my friend Ed has been the most impressive personal example of this type of kingdom-focused leadership. Ed has lived his life using his ability to make money in the oil business to further the kingdom of God. If you talked with him, he would not express these principles as I have written them, but he has lived them. Ed's legacy is his desire to allow God to work in his life and through his life and to watch for spiritual opportunities to advance the kingdom. He has been a mentor, friend, advisor, and father to me. But most all, he is an example of a kingdom-focused leader.

I hope to live the rest of my life practicing the things I have communicated in this book. There is no way to measure the impact a kingdom-focused leader can have on a church, a business, an organization, a community, or the world. Live your life in the three dimensions of the kingdom of God. Focus your attention on the kingdom; make it your desire to further the kingdom of God regardless of the personal cost to you. Live at full capacity as a kingdom-focused leader! "Seek first the kingdom of God and His righteousness, and all these things will be provided for you" (Matt. 6:33).

Endnotes

Chapter 1, What's a Leader to Do?

1. Gene Mims, *The Kingdom-Focused Church* (Nashville: Broadman & Holman, 2003), ix.

2. Charles R. Swindoll, *Living Above the Level of Mediocrity* (Nashville: Word Publishing Group, 1987, 1989), 33–35.

3. Merrill J. Oster and Mike Hamel, *The Entrepreneur's Creed: The Principles and Passions of 20 Successful Entrepreneurs* (Nashville: Broadman & Holman, 2001), 18.

4. Ibid.

5. Dallas Willard, *The Spirit of the Disciplines* (San Francisco: Harper Collins, 1990), 214.

Chapter 2, The Big Picture—The Kingdom of God

1. Janice Miller, *This Blue Planet: Finding God in the Wonders of Nature* (Chicago: Moody Press, 1994), 21.

2. Ibid., 66.

3. Henry T. Blackaby and Claude V. King, *Experiencing God: Knowing and Doing the Will of God* (Nashville: LifeWay Press, 1990), 15.

4. Tertullian, *Apologeticus.* c. 50, quoted in John Bartlett, *Familiar Quotations,* 10th ed., 1919. Available on the Internet: *www.bartleby.com.*

Chapter 3, Who's in Charge?

1. Oster and Hamel, *Entrepreneur's Creed,* 68–69.

2. Christopher A. Crane and Mike Hamel, *Executive Influence: Impacting Your Workplace for Christ* (Colorado Springs: NavPress, 2003), 26.

3. Ibid., 21.

Chapter 5, The Kingdom in You—Responding to God's Call

1. Oster and Hamel, *Entrepreneur's Creed.* 11.

2. Max Lucado, *Just Like Jesus* (Nashville: Word Publishing, 1998), 3.

3. Gene Wilkes, *My Identity in Christ* (Nashville: LifeWay Press, 1997), 16–17. The Os Guinness quotation is from *The Call: Finding and Fulfilling the Central Purpose of Your Life* (Nashville: Word Publishing Group, 1998), 29.

4. Wilkes, *Identity,* 45–46.

5. Mike and Debi Rogers, *The Kingdom Agenda: Experiencing God in Your Workplace* (Nashville: LifeWay Press, 1997), 16–17.

Chapter 6, The Kingdom in You—Developing Christlike Character

1. Bill Hybels, *Who You Are When No One's Looking* (Downers Grove, Ill.: InterVarsity Press, 1987), 7–8.

2. James M. Kouzes and Barry Z. Posner, *Credibility: How Leaders Gain and Lose It, Why People Demand It* (San Francisco: Jossey-Bass, 1993), 13–18.

3. Oster and Hamel, *Entrepreneur's Creed,* 127.

Chapter 7, The Kingdom Through You

1. Mike Rogers, "Church Members in the Marketplace: How to Develop Influential Leaders," *Church Administration,* Summer 2001, 6–9.

2. Ibid.

3. Ibid.

4. Ibid.

Chapter 8, The Kingdom Around You

1. Blackaby and King, *Experiencing God,* 15.